Anna Shipton

Waymarks of my Pilgrimage

Poems

Anna Shipton

Waymarks of my Pilgrimage
Poems

ISBN/EAN: 9783337293116

Printed in Europe, USA, Canada, Australia, Japan

Cover: Foto ©Thomas Meinert / pixelio.de

More available books at **www.hansebooks.com**

Waymarks of my Pilgrimage.

POEMS.

BY

ANNA SHIPTON,

AUTHOR OF

"*The Watch-Tower in the Wilderness,*" "*Wayside Service,*"
"*Asked of God,*" "*The Promise and The Promiser,*"
"*Tell Jesus,*" etc.

"THE LORD IS MY STRENGTH AND MY SHIELD; MY HEART TRUSTED
IN HIM, AND I AM HELPED: THEREFORE MY HEART GREATLY
REJOICETH; AND WITH MY SONG WILL I PRAISE HIM."
Psalm xxviii. 7.

LONDON: MORGAN AND SCOTT,
(OFFICE OF "The Christian,")
12, PATERNOSTER BUILDINGS. E.C.
And may be ordered of any Bookseller.

UNTO

THE LEADER OF ISRAEL,

"WISE IN HEART, AND MIGHTY IN STRENGTH,"

I COMMIT THESE "WAYMARKS OF MY PILGRIMAGE,"

PRAYING HIM

TO COMMAND A BLESSING ON THEM

FOR HIS NAME'S SAKE.

PREFACE.

"Thou shalt remember all the way which the Lord thy God led thee these forty years in the wilderness, to humble thee, and to prove thee, to know what was in thine heart, whether thou wouldest keep His commandments, or no. And he humbled thee, and suffered thee to hunger, and fed thee with manna, which thou knewest not, neither did thy fathers know; that he might make thee know that man doth not live by bread only, but by every word that proceedeth out of the mouth of the Lord doth man live."—*Deut.* viii. 2, 3.

"EVERY place whereon the soles of your feet shall tread shall be yours." (Deut. xi. 24.) This promise was not given to a band of stalwart warriors, but to a people who were without strength, the fewest in number of all people, and in the sight of the world to-day no more than Israel of old in the presence of the Syrian army, even as "two little flocks of kids." (1 Kings xx. 27.)

Every circumstance of our daily life that reveals more of God in Christ—His infinite holiness and power, His infinite love and wisdom—becomes experimentally a component part of our inalienable inheritance. Let us not be slack to go forward to possess the land which the Lord God of our fathers hath given us. Trial and temptation, obstacles and conflicts, on our way, tend to this end, that we "may know Him" (1 John v. 20), and "to give the light of the knowledge of the glory of God in the face of Jesus Christ." (2 Cor. iv. 6.) As our sinfulness and insufficiency are disclosed by the work of the Holy Spirit, so the sufficiency of the Lord Jesus to meet all our needs is unfolded through our personal dealing with the Lord Himself, by whom alone we have access to the Father.

The promise to the Church in the wilderness stands good for God's Israel to-day: "I will dwell among the children of Israel, and will be their God. And they shall know that I am the Lord their God, that brought them forth out of the land of Egypt. I am the Lord their God." (Exod. xxix. 45, 46.)

The land through which we march to-day is a land of hills and valleys, and drinketh of the dew of heaven; with enemies without and within; but "the Lord will be the hope of His people, the strength of the children of Israel." We have had our Marahs and our Rephaims, our Elims and our Jehovahjirehs; and over every landmark of His love we set up our Ebenezer, and declare that God is faithful from the first promise that marked our wandering way to the last.

Perhaps, like Jacob, spiritually slothful, absorbed by care, or by zeal without knowledge, we have forgotten our Bethel rest and Bethel vows, until a thorn in our nest has become a message from the Lord to bring us back by the way that we went; not for rebuke, but blessing.

None but the angels witnessed the first manifestation of His favour; but the ladder of promise shines like the morning star in its lambent glory in our past, and, returning to the place where God has called us, the same bright witnesses of our awakening welcome us in the way that we should go. Henceforth we have not only a Bethel to record, but a Mahanaim we never looked for.

But who shall declare the hour when even the blessing of Bethel waned before the sunrise of glory, and we passed over Peniel from the manifested presence of the Lord Himself, whom we were so slow to seek of our own will? He giveth more than we ask, more than the heart of man can conceive. He pitieth as a Father, He giveth as a King!

We are every day writing our life on tables more enduring than stone. It is not read by those who misunderstand us, nor in the partial comprehension that may win the approbation or censure of men, but it is that which stands before God, of which He alone is cognizant, flowing from the Spirit, or the works of the flesh—indestructible records which influence others, for good or evil, through eternal ages. It is a deeply solemn thought; and but for the knowledge of Him who is our strength and our life, for the ever-open Fountain of Israel, the traveller may well shrink with dismay.

The *anointed* waymarks of our pilgrimage are among the precious things separated from the vile, on which we may look back, while giving glory to God, as we press onward towards the prize of our high calling.

The natural man would fain forget the trials of the way, but we have not so learned Christ. Our faithlessness and fears record His tenderness; our sins and iniquities, that He remembers no more, mark the grace and wisdom of a loving Father's chastening; the conflict in which the Captain of our salvation taught our hands to war and our fingers to fight strengthens faith in Him in the battle to-day; and even the scar of the wound He healed is endeared to us by the sympathy of Him who loveth at all times.

The following pages are for the most part such waymarks of my journey home, very inadequately recording the abounding consolations in Christ, or the fulfilment of His inexhaustible promises, nevertheless embalming for my own encouragement the blessed remembrance of lovingkindness and tender mercies. They have been scattered in various works; but as they may not all come under the notice of those for whom this little volume is intended, I have gathered them as far as I have been able, knowing that what God has blessed is for ever, and praying Him that others may share the light that shone in desert places, for the least of the family of God, and dig for themselves "in the everlasting hills" for "the unsearchable riches of Christ."

August, 1877.

CONTENTS.

	PAGE
"All things are yours!" Yea, Lord, I know it	5
A minstrel went to a rich man's door	146
Are the burdens that press thee thus sorely?	76
Arise, and take courage!	45
As wearily I wandered on a day	22
Behold a messenger, my Lord	133
Be still, O Jordan's billows!	96
"Call them in," the poor, the wretched, sin-stained wanderers from the fold	144
Christ, the Fountain of my blessing	106
Come, ye toiling hearts that labour	83
Dark the way I wander	113
Far upon the shining shore	109
Green pastures in the wilderness	36
God bless thee to-day with joy that never	142
God lives! Then why should I despond?	85
Halt! another milestone	18
He was better to me than all my hopes	120
Hush thou thy sigh! Rebellious heart, be still!	67
I did not ask Him for a harp	37
I leave Thee, Lord, my jewels	41
I looked upon the olive-grove	8
I praise Thee, O my Father	104
I said, "Where shall I flee?"	56
I saw a taper's light	80
I wait for Thee, Beloved	21
I wept by the misty headland	30
I will stand alone on my watch-tower	63
I would have asked a smoother road	123
If only in life's pleasant ways	54
If this Thy promise, gracious Lord	52
In the wondrous breastplate golden	111
In this home of heavenly mansions	115

Contents.

	PAGE
It was the hour of battle	14
"Jesus is here and yonder"	118
Keep thy watch, it is daybreak	91
Leading me by ways I know not	34
"Let us go forth!" and leave the world behind us	1
Lord, hide me in Thy shadow	47
Lord! I fain would love Thee more	82
Lord, I would work for Thee	71
Lord, in Thy presence let me hide	77
"Lovest thou Me?"	55
Make me, Lord, as a fountain	27
My plea is not my love, Lord	79
My soul is dark and dumb! Why is it, Lord?	135
Oh, buy the field, the priceless field	73
Oh, fierce the foes that never tire	101
Oh for a priceless crown of stars!	94
Oh, tarry not, and look not thou behind thee!	74
O Lamb of God, I know that Thou art here!	132
O Lord, my God, by Thee	90
Once I said: O Master, tell me	2
On to the Refuge!—straight it lies before you	59
Sad is my heart, and dark as cold	78
Saw ye my soul's Beloved?	66
Say not, "He answered nothing." Thou didst pray	7
See, the sun is sinking	140
See where the sunlight falls	93
Shall I see my risen Saviour?	60
Shall I shrink and be afraid?	20
So far with me, no farther now	89
The freed bird from its cage hath fled	50
The little flock! Lord, fetch them home	29
The wilderness way I wandered	10
There's many a record written	4
There passed along a weary man	107
Thou art my Refuge, Lord. I flee	138
Thou hast been Home and Friend in deserts lonely	53
Thou hast but claimed Thine own; Lord, I surrender	68
Thou knowest, Lord, Thou knowest all about me	35
Thou, who hast my sins forgiven	58
Under the shadow of thy boughs	103
Up, mourning soul! though shadows round thee hover	70
We laid our darling in the dust	84
We leave, Lord, in Thy keeping	124
We listened to the voices	126
Welcome the darkness, for Thou art near	33
When the Father His little one smiteth	87
With Him for ever! O my soul, look forth	28

WAYMARKS OF MY PILGRIMAGE.

"*LET US GO FORTH!*"

"Let us go forth therefore unto Him without the camp, bearing His reproach."—*Heb.* xiii. 13.

"To him that overcometh will I grant to sit with Me in My throne, even as I also overcame, and am set down with My Father in His throne. He that hath an ear, let him hear what the Spirit saith unto the churches."—*Rev.* iii. 21, 22.

"LET us go forth!" and leave the world behind us,
 And meet the perils of the pilgrim way;
Where Jesus leads, let mocking scoffers find us
 Still hastening onward, as they bid us stay.

"Let us go forth!" and tell the same sweet story,
 How Christ for us a helpless Babe became;
Point to the dying Lamb, the Lord of glory,
 Strong in the might that lives in Jesus' Name.

"Let us go forth!" The pilgrim and the stranger
    Owns not the earth his weary foot must tread;
God's sinless Son, once pillowed in the manger,
    Had not below whereon to lay His head.

"Let us go forth!" Where Jesus walked before us,
    Unmoved by praise or censure's fleeting breath,
God's eye of love is fondly watching o'er us,
    The arms Eternal stretching underneath.

"Let us go forth!" Without the camp there liveth
    The Strength of Israel! Ye of heavenly birth,
Bask in the smile the loving Master giveth
    To them that follow Him. "Let us go forth!"

RETURNING.

"Jesus beholding him loved him, and said unto him, One thing thou lackest."—Mark x. 21.

ONCE I said: O Master, tell me
    How Thy kingdom to attain;
What shall fit me for Thy presence?
    How Thy favour may I gain?

"Leave," He said, "thy rich possessions;
    Come, and thou shalt fitted be
For the kingdom of My Father:
    Take thy cross, and follow Me."

Then I turned me full of sorrow,
  Counting up life's precious store;
For I knew not all the idols
  Cherished in my heart before.

But the Saviour looked upon me,
  And He loved me; oh, how well!
Love awaked new life within me,
  Light upon my spirit fell.

Then how poor were my possessions,
  And my treasures mean and dim:
Jesus Christ had smiled upon me:
  I returned and followed Him.

O my Lord! Thy smile was favour,
  Though on my cold heart it shone;
And Thy love is life eternal:
  So my wandering heart was won.

SONGS IN THE NIGHT.

"Where is God my Maker, who giveth songs in the night?"
Job xxxv. 10.

THERE'S many a record written
   We cannot read aright;
But let us praise the Giver
   Of a new song in the night.

We'll praise Him for the mercies
   That marked our homeward way;
For the stars that cheered our midnight,
   And the sun that makes our day.

For many a word of comfort,
   Like manna on the dew;
And many a tender greeting,
   From loyal heart and true.

For many a love-sent message,
   Carried by wind and wave;
And many a golden promise,
   Though floating o'er a grave.

Not in this land of shadows
   We read the road aright;
But never yet hath failed me,
   A sweet song in the night.

THE GOLDEN SCEPTRE.

"What wilt thou, Queen Esther? and what is thy request?"
Esther v. 3.
"This is the confidence that we have in Him, that, if we ask anything according to His will, He heareth us."
I *John* v. 14.
"All things are yours."—I *Cor.* iii. 21.

"ALL things are yours!" Yea, Lord, I know it;
    But oh, how cold my heart must be
    To doubt the love that can bestow it,
    And tarry still afar from Thee!

I claim Thy promise while I plead it;
    Behold, I take Thee at Thy word;
    Thou seest how much to-day I need it:
    Help for the helpless, gracious Lord!

Look on my sick, my dumb, my dying,
    Touch Thou my blind that they may see;
    This broken heart, in anguish sighing:
    I bring them one and all to Thee.

My heart's best treasures, here I give them,
　　To be within Thy temple stored;
And as life's landmarks there I leave them,
　　"Because I asked [them] of the Lord."

When love would fail in fruitless yearning,
　　Thy golden censer wafts my prayers;
I see the perfumed incense burning:
　　All things are mine, all things are theirs.

I bring the care, sharp and oppressing;
　　The way perplexed; the path untrod;
This feeble service for Thy blessing,
　　Oh crown it, "Given thee of God!"

I ask for patience, faith, and meekness,
　　And love divine that all endures:
Give me Thy strength to meet my weakness,
　　Since Thou hast said, "All things are yours."

I bring the sin my soul distressing,
　　That Thou mayst cleanse me pure and white;
The faint foreboding past expressing,
　　But clear before Thy searching sight.

Oh, let me feel Thee ever nigh me,
　　And seek Thy smile all gifts above!
No good thing will Thy grace deny me,
　　The object of Thy changeless love.

Thus shall I tread the roaring billow,
  Looking to Him who hears it roar;
Thy hand my guide, Thy breast my pillow,
  Lord, let me trust, and doubt no more!

Safe in the bark Thou bad'st me enter,
  I'll triumph in Thy power divine;
And on Thy word my all I venture,
  For Thou hast said, "All things are mine."

SILENCE.

"He answered her not a word. . . . O woman, great is thy faith: be it unto thee even as thou wilt."
Matt. xv. 23, 28.

SAY not, "He answered nothing." Thou didst pray,
"Give me Thyself! and lo! He takes away
Thine idol from thy fond arms' fevered fold;
His garment's hem thy failing fingers hold.
Hush! in that solemn silence He hath heard
Thy sob of anguish and each faltering word;
Go, plead again, and yet again: thy need
Is what thy Saviour meteth; therefore plead.
What! still He answereth nothing! Nay; beneath
That silence rolls, "O woman, great thy faith!"

THE LOOK.

"The Lord looked upon him, and said, Go in this thy might."—Judges vi. 14.

LOOKED upon the olive-grove,
    What comfort could it bring?
The fruitful vine, once full of speech,
    Was but a common thing.
Up to the gorgeous skies I gazed,
    Down to the silvery sea,
On to the purple sunset heights;
    But all were dumb to me.

Then back I turned to vanished days,
    When Christ His love revealed:
To messages of hope and peace
    His faithful hand had sealed.
And well I knew, "for me He died,"
    But yet no rest could be,
Until my drooping heart could sing,
    "My Saviour lives for me."

I looked upon my wounded feet,
    So often led astray;
I strove to count my countless sins,
    For ever put away;

I looked on everything but Him,
  In desolating grief,
And found!—O heart, what couldst thou find
  Of solace and relief?

Then sat I down before the Lord,
  That He my need might see;
And helpless, hopeless, speechless, there
  My Saviour looked on me.
Oh, look of life! oh, might of love!
  My heart that glance returned,
And melting 'neath His heavenly smile,
  With joy and ardour burned.

Just so my sweet and sovereign Lord
  On Peter looked before:
He, in the strength of that one look,
  Denied his Lord no more;
But followed Him in life to death:
  Lord, let me do the same;
Yea, let me go in this Thy might—
  Strong in Thy holy Name.

MELIORA.

"The disciple is not above his Master."—*Luke* vi. 40.
"That no man should be moved by these afflictions: for yourselves know that we are appointed thereunto."
1 *Thess.* iii. 3.

THE wilderness way I wandered
   Had many a valley and hill;
When I heard a song in the silence:
   Its melody lingereth still.
It breathed o'er my sinking spirit—
   "Meliora! Child, look up!
Follow thy Master's footsteps;
   Drink of thy Master's cup."

Sadly I smiled as I answered—
   "How can I follow Him now?
The light is gone from the mountain,
   And wildly the night winds blow.
I wield no sword for our Leader;
   No banner my weak hands hold:
I but clasp it close to my bosom,
   And hide in its crimson fold."

" Droop not to-day.   Meliora !
    Drink of the chalice He fills :
Grace is laid up for the weakest,
    Strength for the service He wills.
' All things are yours ;' yea, the glory,
    The darkness, the desert, to-day ;
And He who hath trod it before thee
    Hath hallowed thy toilsome way.

" Fight 'gainst the power of evil ;
    Up to the girded race !
Each hath a charge in the temple,
    All in the kingdom a place.
Wait where thy Master hath called thee,
    Patiently suffer His will ;
Enough, oh, enough, if He bade thee
    Be silent, and helpless, and still.

" Brave hearts fall in the battle,
    The race and the chaplet won ;
And some with the standard flying
    Must rally the ranks alone ;
Some lie on the wayside wounded,
    And some with their Leader rest :
Who doeth the will of the Father
    Serveth the Master best.

"So keep thy watch at the portal;
   The Master hath bid thee wait,
And speak the word that He gives thee,
   As wanderers pass the gate.
When the sneer of the scoffer moves thee,
   Meliora! Child, look up!
Follow thy Master's footsteps;
   Drink of thy Master's cup.

"A vessel meet for His service
   The Potter must frame and mould;
There's the fining-pot for the silver,
   And the furnace-flame for the gold:
But One watches o'er the fire—
   A watch that thou canst not share;
Look up! Look up! Meliora!
   The Lord whom thou lov'st is there."

Over the world's wide waters
   The dove could her message bring;
And still at our curtained casement
   A minstrel waiteth to sing.
There's many a bird at the threshold
   Who bringeth a song in the night;
And we praise the love that hath lent him,
   As we follow his upward flight.

Thus often my night-watch keeping,
  In moments with sadness fraught,
Sweet words to my drooping spirit
  Have the billows of ocean brought.
Greetings from heavenly kindred
  I never on earth shall see,
And blessings from friends long parted
  Are songs like my bird's to me.

And low they sing, "Meliora!
  The journey is shortening home;
To-night we are nearer the Glory,
  And brighter the days to come.
Secure in the arms that bear thee,
  Meliora! take thy rest:
Who doeth the will of the Father
  Serveth the Master best."

THE WOUNDED SOLDIER.

"The soul of the wounded crieth out: yet God layeth not folly to them."—Job xxiv. 12.

It was the hour of battle,
   No human eye looked on;
Angels and devils, marvel;
   A victory is won!

There is a moan of anguish,
   A warrior lies low;
A poisoned shaft is proving
   The malice of the foe.

In the still midnight hour
   No other sound is heard
The weary hands fall helpless
   That wielded well the sword.

There is no song of triumph,
   And none the chaplet twine,
O weak and wounded soldier,
   For that pale brow of thine.

Hath earth no balm to bring him?
  Hath love no word to speak,
As in the dust he lieth,
  With heart so nigh to break?

For fierce the foe that found him,
  (And who his power can scan?)
Oh, is there none to succour
  That sad and lonely man?

Not earth, with all its glories
  Could solace now impart;
Nor earthly love, the dearest,
  Uphold that sinking heart.

But see! the Man of Sorrows
  Comes where His soldier lies;
He marks the lip that quivers
  In untold agonies.

Say, doth He bring him fetters,
  Or comes He to upbraid?
Nay! to the rest that fails not
  He draws the drooping head.

And in that deep, deep silence
  The gaping wounds are bound,
With touch so soft and gentle—
  Hush! it is holy ground.

O Christ! Thy tender pity
   For every pang I see;
Each sob of pain is numbered,
   And counted as for Thee.

Yea, closer, and yet closer,
   Thy wounded one is prest;
And human woes are whispered
   Upon a human breast.

Then in the solemn silence
   I hear the whisper sweet,
"Fear not, My wounded soldier;
   Behold My hands and feet!"

*   *   *   *   *   *

The fever dream is over;
   The tearless eyes can weep;
And He, whose arms enfold him,
   Gives His beloved sleep.

Rest, rest, O wounded soldier!
   Distrust thy Lord no more;
And think not strange the battle
   Thy Captain fought before.

He knows thy fierce accuser;
    Thou shalt not fall nor yield;
Hold fast thy blood-red banner,
    Thy bright sword, and thy shield.

Behold thy strength in Jesus;
    Believe thy Brother nigh,
Whose heart in love o'erfloweth
    With tenderest sympathy.

Thou hast no pain He feels not,
    No pang He cannot share;
And when the fight was hottest,
    Deliverance was near.

He kept thee in the conflict;
    His shield was o'er thee thrown;
A Conqueror ne'er defeated,
    Thy battle was His own.

Rest in His love, and fear not;
    The victory is won.
O weak and wounded soldier,
    Thy Lord hath said, "Well done!"

THE GOLDEN PROMISE.

"Lo, I am with you alway, even unto the end of the world."
Matt. xxviii. 20.
"Man doth not live by bread only, but by every word that proceedeth out of the mouth of the Lord doth man live."
Deut. viii. 3.

HALT! another milestone
Marks the road I travel;
Dark the desert pathway
Still before me lies.
He who bade me follow,
Strength and light bestoweth
For that homeward journey
Hidden from my eyes.
"I will never leave thee,"
Echoes o'er the mountain;
"I will ne'er forsake thee;"
Trust the word He saith.
"For this God is our God for ever and ever;
He will be our Guide even unto death."

Past the pathless river
Deserts lie beyond me;
Cloud and fiery pillar
Lead me on alone.
Fountains fresh, and manna,
Tell who goes before me;

Elims wait my weariness
When my journey's done.
Christ Himself is smiling
On each faint endeavour.
Forward! through the desert;
On from faith to faith.
"For this God is our God for ever and ever;
He will be our Guide even unto death."

Thorns and briers may wound me,
He is near to heal me,
Near to fight my battle,
Put to flight my foe;
Near to cleanse my garments
If I careless wander;
Near to sweeten Marah
All the way I go.
Trust Him, only trust Him;
Who the bond can sever?
Feebly may I follow,
But follow still in faith.
"For this God is our God for ever and ever;
He will be our Guide even unto death."

Halt! anoint the milestone
With the oil of gladness;
Rest awhile and ponder
On the unseen way.

Praise shall bring our blessings
Down the angels' ladder;
And the golden promise
Turn our night to day.
"Speak, Thy servant heareth;"
Henceforth let me follow,
Let me trust the living God,
And every word He saith.
" For this God is our God for ever and ever;
He will be our Guide even unto death."

THE ROCK OF MY HEART.

"Fear not; I will help thee."—*Isaiah* xli. 13.

HALL I shrink and be afraid?
"I will help thee," Christ hath said.
Shall I flee before the foe
When His arm can lay him low?
  Jesus! Rock of strength divine,
  Be my watchword, "Christ is mine."

Shall I sigh for cisterns here,
When a fountain floweth near?
Shall I carry life's sad weight,
Weeping o'er my lost estate?
  Nay! salvation's might shall shine
  In my watchword, "Christ is mine."

SUNRISE.

"I will come again, and receive you unto myself; that where I am, there ye may be also."—*John* xiv. 3.

I WAIT for Thee, Beloved,
   I watch for Thee to come;
Away from night's dark shadows,
   Soon wilt Thou guide me home.

Hush! for I know the dawning
   Is surely drawing near;
Speak softly, let me listen,
   His welcome voice I hear.

He cometh! my Beloved,
   Yet blind eyes cannot see
The glory of His coming;
   But I know He comes for me.

*   *   *   *   *

Ah! it is dark no longer,
   I knew He could not fail;
Death hath for me no terror,
   There's sunrise in the vale.

WHISPERS 'NEATH THE PALMS.

"And when they had platted a crown of thorns, they put it upon His head, and a reed in His right hand."
Matt. xxvii. 29.
"We have this treasure in earthen vessels, that the excellency of the power may be of God, and not of us. . . . Always bearing about in the body the dying of the Lord Jesus, that the life also of Jesus might be made manifest in our body."—2 *Cor.* iv. 7, 10.

AS wearily I wandered on a day,
Where noiselessly the yellow Nile sweeps by,
I rested 'neath a Palm, whose branches spread
Their dark green leaves against the glowing sky.

Bright flashed the light o'er minaret and dome,
And the blue desert seemed a pathless shore
To fairer temples builded in the sky,
Of every rainbow hue that clouds e'er wore.

Vainly I listened for the Palm's sweet song:
Her golden crown was glist'ning in the sun,
And down the stately bole the rippling rays
Seemed like a molten rivulet to run.

But all was silence round me, silence deep;
    The wind's hot breath the feathery foliage stirred;
But that blest Name, all other names above,
    In whispered harmony I never heard.

Just so Thy Praise, Lord, slumbered in my soul,
    Waiting the Holy Spirit's quickening might;
Sleeping for sadness till Thy south wind came
    To wake Thy garden into life and light.

A few frail reeds and rushes fringed the shore,
    Their bloom and verdure gone, broken and dry,
Fit emblem of a helpless, lifeless thing:
    O gracious Master, such a one am I!

I watched the white doves pass me in their flight,
    And longed for such fleet pinions to be free,
So to escape this stormy wilderness,
    And rest for ever, Lord, with Thee—with Thee!

Mourning, I bowed beside that turbid wave,
    Like the poor reed parched in the summer drought,
And learned again a lesson conned before,
    Of base things, things despised, and things of nought.

For softer than the wild dove's plaintive note,
    Or voice of many waters, gently stole
The tender chiding of a wounded Friend,
    And its low whisper shook my prostrate soul.

"And wilt *thou* also go away, while yet
    The whitened fields await the golden morn?
'Canst thou not watch with Me one little hour,'
    To cheer some wanderer, weary and forlorn?"

And then I answered, "Lord, no skill have I:
    My hand is feeble, and my spirit quails.
Let me lie down in silence at Thy feet;
    Weary and faint, at last my courage fails."

"Child, wouldst thou rest while yet the Master waits?
    Droop in the race before the crown is won?
Escape the shame, the burden, and the toil,
    And lose the seed-time ere thy work be done?"

"I am not learned, Lord, I have no strength;
    And if I have, it wars against Thy will.
Thou bid'st me wait, and I am full of care;
    Thou call'st me forward, and behold me, still!"

"I am thy Strength; and thou shalt live to praise
    For all the way I led thee. Why repine?
Be of good courage, 'tis My word thou bear'st;
    Be thine the willing heart, the power is Mine."

"My harp is all unstrung; my only song
    Is, like the palm-tree's, folded in a word;
And e'en my praise is stammered more than sung,
    My coward heart lies low—Thou know'st it, Lord!

"Oh, were I like yon fair and fruitful Palm,
   Glory and pleasure Thou wouldst find in me;
Gath'ring the warmth and light from heaven alone,
   I'd bear my golden fruit, a crown for Thee!"

"Patience, poor weary one! The lofty Palm,
   That by the waters spreads its thirsty root,
Is not more fair in its Creator's eyes
   Than the bruised reed beneath thy careless foot.

"Did they not crown thy Master's brow with thorns,
   And lead Him forth to die—yea, die for thee—
Surrounded by the scoffing multitude,
   That in false homage bent the mocking knee?

"Hast thou not wept, while pondering on that hour?
   I know thou hast. But didst thou never heed
How in His hand, the right Hand of His power,
   They thrust a sceptre?—'twas a feeble reed.

"They knew not what they did; but thou hast known.
   Why art thou troubled? Why this sore distress?
For that frail sceptre still shall bruise the foe,
   And carry comfort to the comfortless.

"They knew not what they did. It is that Hand
   That now upholds thee, lest thou fly, or yield:
Cast then thy weakness on Almighty power;
   I am thy sure reward, thy Sun and Shield."

"Oh, cleanse the vessel Thou hast emptied, Lord,
And make me meet to bear the oil and wine!
It is enough to be a thing of nought:
The might and glory, Lord, be Thine—all Thine!"

[NOTE.—It is an Oriental tradition, that the palm branches, when they quiver in the wind, whisper the name which is above all other names—"JESUS." The only traveller I have met who ever listened for it was a Christian officer, who told me he had slept beneath a group of these interesting trees, so full of Scripture emblems, and on his waking he thought there was no difficulty in imagining the sound of a Hebrew word produced by the morning breeze sweeping through the long palm-leaves. To him its voice was "Ishi." (Hosea ii. 16.)]

"STREAMS THAT MAKE GLAD THE CITY OF OUR GOD."

"Whosoever drinketh of the water that I shall give him shall never thirst; but the water that I shall give him shall be in him a well of water springing up into everlasting life."
John iv. 14.
"He that believeth on Me, as the Scripture hath said, out of his belly shall flow rivers of living water."—*John* vii. 38.

MAKE me, Lord, as a fountain,
   Spring from the depths below!
Far in channels of blessing
   The waters of life may flow;
Soft as the night-dew falling,
   Swift as the carrier dove,
Bearing my Master's message,
   Telling my Saviour's love:

Springing up in the sunshine,
   Glad in its dazzling light,
Cheering the heart-sick watcher,
   Whispering songs in the night;
Loving the stars that lightened
   The drops that in sadness fell,
Ever fresh springs rise in the darkness,
   Deep from the fathomless well.

  Then to run as a river—
   A river of truth and joy—
  A river to flow for ever,
   When cisterns of earth are dry,
  Bearing a brother's burden
   Over the dark world's flood,
  Filling a thousand fountains
   To gladden the City of God.

"*FOR EVER WITH THE LORD.*"

WITH Him for ever! O my soul, look forth
  From the dim lattice! Pleasures without end
Wait thee to-morrow. One of matchless worth
Hath sought and loved thee, and hath called thee
  "Friend."

For ever with Thee! Let me then rejoice,
  Waiting and watching till I see Thee come,
And hear the summons of Thy well-known voice,
  To mount Thy chariot to my happy home.
Now teach me, Lord, in all my care, to see
Thy love unfolding; all Thy care for me.

THE SCATTERED FLOCK.

"And other sheep I have, which are not of this fold : them also I must bring, and they shall hear My voice ; and there shall be one fold, and one Shepherd."—*John* x. 16.

THE little flock ! Lord, fetch them home ;
   Draw them to follow Thee ;
Thou seest how far the ramblers rove,
   And where the slumberers be.
Some have set forth at early dawn,
   And now are wandering wide ;
And others, wounded by the way,
   Faint by the green hill-side.

Lord, bring them home ! and we will go
   Forth at Thy blest command,
And seek Thy weary sheep for Thee
   In this wide stranger land.
But go Thou with us. Go before,
   And keep Thy watch above ;
Thy banished to the fold restore,
   The fruit of deathless love.

"*MY INFIRMITY.*"

"He that spared not His own Son, but delivered Him up for us all, how shall He not with Him also freely give us all things?"—*Rom.* viii. 32.
"Hath God forgotten to be gracious? hath He in anger shut up His tender mercies? And I said, This is my infirmity."
Psalm lxxvii. 9, 10.

WEPT by the misty headland,
  Down by the sea;
And none in that hour of anguish
  Stood there by me.
Within and without was midnight;
  Where once had been
The smile of the Lord who loved me,
  No Lord was seen.

I said, "On this earth's wide bosom
  I walk alone;
God hideth His face, I'm forsaken;
  All hope is gone.
I watch for His hand in the shadows
  That shroud my feet;
I listen, and nothing I hear, save
  My heart's wild beat.

"Cold, drear, is my soul, and loveless,
  Hopeless and dead;
For God has departed for ever,"
  Sadly I said.
"I shall never more bask in His presence,
  Never proclaim,
With a song and the voice of thanksgiving,
  Jesus' sweet Name.

"Yet how can I marvel He leaves me,
  Faithless and vain,
To walk in the light of His favour
  Never again!
My heart hath forsaken His mercies,
  And mercy is past,
And my Lord, whom my sins have long wearied,
  Leaves me at last."

Then, swift as the flash of the lightning
  Passing the sky,
Came a voice, like a dove's in the woodland,
  So tenderly:
"When father and mother forsake thee,
  Look thou above;
The Father Eternal remembers
  The child of His love.

"The shadows have gathered around thee,
    Born of the light;
Had the sun never risen to warm thee,
    Where were thy night?
Remember the springs in the desert,
    Arid and drear;
For thee hath the wilderness blossomed,
    Why dost thou fear?

"There are treasures beneath the dark waters;
    Seek thou, and learn;
Hidden riches in secret places
    Thou must discern.
And think not He changes or chides thee;
    Comforts decline;
But Christ made the covenant blessings
    Eternally thine.

"He gave thee His promise to keep thee;
    Can He deceive?
He granted His Word and His Spirit;
    Only believe.
He sought thee, cast out and forsaken,
    Bidding thee 'Live.'
He gave thee the Son of His bosom;
    More can He give?"

Then swift on the purple headland,
  Down by the sea,
The light that seemed vanished for ever
  Came back to me;
And I looked on the Man Christ Jesus
  On God's high throne.
Forgive me, my Father; I measured
  Thy love by my own.

HEAVENLY GALES.

"Awake, O north wind; and come, thou south; blow upon my garden, that the spices thereof may flow out."
Sol. Song iv. 16.

WELCOME the darkness, for Thou art near;
Welcome the silence, Thy voice I hear;
Welcome the sickness that brought Thee nigh;
Welcome the grief and perplexity.
Better to weep and suffer with Thee,
Than bask in all earth's prosperity.

Welcome the dawn that foretells the day;
The night with its darkness hath passed away;
Welcome the pruning from Thy dear hand.
Let the spices flow that Thy breath hath fanned.
The garden and fruit, it is all Thine own;
The rain is over, the winter is gone.

THE ROCK OF MY STRENGTH.

"Come, see a Man, which told me all things that ever I did: is not this the Christ?"—John iv. 29.

LEADING me by ways I know not,
    O'er the mountain, o'er the wave;
Pitiful in my distresses,
    And in danger swift to save;
Soothing, healing, with a word—
That's my Saviour! That's my Lord!

Faithful when the fondest leave me,
    Nearest when no strength have I,
Tenderest when my brethren grieve me;
    And in each perplexity,
Friend and brother I can claim,
Linked with Jesus' sacred Name.

Washed by Him from sin's defilement,
    Clothed in garments fresh and fair,
Sandals braced for life's long journey,
    And His hand to guide me there;
Saved and sheltered by His blood—
That's my Saviour! That's my God!

Kingdoms and a crown await me
  When my pilgrim journey's done;
But the glory that I covet
  Is to gaze on God's dear Son,
While from heaven's high vault shall ring—
"That's my Saviour! That's my King!"

"THOU KNOWEST THY SERVANT."

THOU knowest, Lord, Thou knowest all about me,
  And all the winding way my feet have trod;
And now Thou know'st I cannot go without Thee
  To guide me onward through the swelling flood.

Thou know'st my way—how lone, how dark, how cheerless,
  If Thy dear hand I fail in all to see;
Bright with Thy smile of love, my heart is fearless
  When in my weakness I can lean on Thee.

Give me Thy presence; go Thou, Lord, before me;
  Make a plain path where all is rough and drear;
So let me trust the Love that watches o'er me,
  And in the shadows still believe Thee near.

THE WAY IN THE DESERT.

"In the daytime also He led them with a cloud, and all the night with a light of fire. He clave the rocks in the wilderness, and gave them drink as out of the great depths."
Psalm lxxviii. 14, 15.

GREEN pastures in the wilderness
   My Shepherd keeps for me;
And rivulets among the rocks
   My blind eyes cannot see.

Weary and faint I travel on
   The road to home and rest;
So let me cast my care on Him:
   My Father knoweth best.

Yea, Heavenly Shepherd, all my care
   I fain to Thee would bring:
For in the wilderness I walk
   Thou seest the secret spring.

The quiet halting-place in view,
   Sweet Elim's sheltered spot,
Where Thou wilt whisper to my heart,
   "Thou hast not been forgot."

VEILED BLESSINGS.

"God thundereth marvellously with His voice; great things doeth He, which we cannot comprehend."—*Job* xxxvii. 5.
"The eyes of them that see shall not be dim, and the ears of them that hear shall hearken."—*Isaiah* xxxii. 3.

DID not ask Him for a harp,
   And yet a harp He gave;
His praise was slumbering in my heart,
   Like whispers 'neath the wave.
The storm hath rent the hidden rock
   Ere from its cave it tore
The pearl and weed the billows cast
   Alike upon the shore.

O wondrous forms of life, that make
   A garden in the deep!
And wondrous echoes, mute erewhile,
   In deep, untroubled sleep,
Until the God of glory spake
   In voice of majesty,
And o'er the many waters rolled
   · Anthems of melody.

So Thou hast tuned the silver strings
    That once Thy tempest wrung,
And bade responsive echoes wake
    In gladness to the song.
And sinking souls have loved the theme;
    Lord, I can bless Thy hand
Which ruled the thunder that awaked
    The chords at Thy command!

Thus pains and perils teach the lore
    That hearts have learned alone,
Interpreting another's woe
    By learning from its own.
I did not ask Thee for a bark,
    Oft storm-tossed on the sea;
I thank Thee now—the billows brought
    Their Lord and mine to me.

Thy presence shed a glory there:
    Thou bad'st my terrors cease,
And whispered to my fainting heart
    Thy covenant of peace.
Weary with care and sorrow, Lord,
    I prayed that I might die;
Thou didst not my petition grant,
    But soothed my bitter cry.

And manifesting all the grace
  Of Thine own heart for me,
Thou bad'st me live, and learn of Him
  Whose love is sympathy.
I thank Thee that Thy wisdom, Lord,
  My heedless prayer denied;
And for my stammering songs of praise,
  A harp Thou hast supplied.

I prayed Thee for a peaceful path,
  Wherever Thou mightst lead;
I pictured pleasant pasture lands
  In Goshen's grassy mead;
I found me in a battle-field,
  Oft wounded and afraid,
That I might learn the art of war,
  And call on Thee for aid.

Then onward, through the wilderness,
  Encamped on barren ground,
I sought and found the hidden springs
  That in Thy love abound;
And bitter waters mocked my thirst,
  That I thenceforth might see
Thou only art the Branch to make
  Life's waters sweet to me.

And when my need hath cried to Thee
    My daily bread to give,
Thou gavest angels' food to me,
    And bade me eat and live.
Importunate and blind, Thou know'st
    How oft Thou wouldst have saved
My foolish heart, that weeping loathed
    The very gifts I craved.

Choose Thou for me! Thy gifts are good,
    Thy way, O Lord, is best;
Grant me Thy presence on my path,
    I leave to Thee the rest.
Still tune my harp to Thy dear name,
    Thy mercies sure to tell
To them who dread the wintry wave,
    Or weep by Marah's well.

CROWN JEWELS.

"The Lord their God shall save them in that day as the flock of His people: for they shall be as the stones of a crown, lifted up as an ensign upon His land."—*Zech.* ix. 16.
"All things come of Thee, and of Thine own have we given Thee."—1 *Chron.* xxix. 14.
"They shall be Mine, saith the Lord of hosts, in that day when I make up My jewels."—*Mal.* iii. 17.

LEAVE Thee, Lord, my jewels,
   Though they are scattered wide;
Have them in Thy close keeping,
   Safe by Thy wounded side.

Thine Eye can still behold them,
   Their place no more I see,
No watch can I keep o'er them,
   Oh, watch o'er them for me!

They are Thine own: I would not
   Adorn myself with them;
Thou hast ordained their beauty
   To grace Thy diadem.

Thy love awhile hath granted
   These "stones of grace" to me:
And now I leave my treasure,
   In trust, O Lord, with Thee!

For some, long time I travailed,
   With many a hope and fear,
And marked them growing brighter
   With each succeeding year.

And some are freshly gathered
   From darksome pit and mine,
By the ensign of Thy power
   In Thy kingly crown to shine.

Fairer than Zion's mountain,
   The eastern sun hath kissed,
Shines in its modest beauty
   Thy purple Amethyst.

By dust of earth encumbered,
   None prized the precious stone;
Christ looked on it, and loved it:
   How fair His gem hath grown.

Here's an Onyx, love-engraven
   By the Master's patient care,
Who reads the secret meaning
   Of each mystic character.

Rough seemed the file and chisel,
   Ordained by Him to bring
New beauty to His jewel,
   More honour to the King.

I wept to see how deeply
    The graver's tool must go;
But now, O God, Thou knowest,
    We would but have it so!

Vainly we watch the seedling
    To life and form expand,
So the work of the great Master
    Is hidden 'neath His Hand.

Here's an Emerald from the valley,
    That suffering endears,
The dearer for the darkness,
    And the waiting, and the tears.

A Diamond from the desert,
    Where I watched all alone;
And a Sapphire, the fairest
    Because my latest one.

There, where the storm raged round us,
    And clouds rolled o'er my head,
I found a rosy Ruby
    Within its sandy bed.

And now it shines in glory,
    More beauteous in Thy sight
Than the golden orb of morning,
    In its radiant car of light.

There's a Topaz—but I leave them,
  My eyes with tears o'erflow;
My heart in love yearns o'er them,
  As Thou alone canst know.

And I would trust Thee fully
  With the dearest gifts I own!
I shall find them in the glory,
  When I see Thee on Thy throne.

In faith and with thanksgiving
  My treasures, Lord, I cast
Upon Thy care, believing
  Their future from my past.

Thy hand alone can fashion
  Thy costly stones to shine;
When Thou makest up Thy jewels—
  No longer mine, but Thine.

BE YE STEDFAST.

"Be ye stedfast, unmoveable, always abounding in the work of the Lord, forasmuch as ye know that your labour is not in vain in the Lord."—1 *Cor.* xv. 58.

ARISE, and take courage!
   Thy Lord goes before thee;
Fight thou the good fight
   For thy God and His glory.
Return to thy fortress
   That cannot be taken,
And rest on thy Rock
   That no earthquake hath shaken.

The waves of destruction
   Shall never come nigh thee;
The danger thou fearest
   Shall harmless pass by thee;
Because thou hast made
   The Lord's name thy salvation,
Thy tower of defence
   In the day of temptation.

Take the strong shield of faith
   That God's soldiers inherit,
The helm of salvation,
   The sword of the Spirit;

Thy loins gird with truth,
   And thy breast guard from evil:
And so shalt thou stand
   'Gainst the wiles of the devil.

Not alone in the combat
   In which thou hast striven;
Look above; for behold there
   The Lamb slain, in heaven.
Then fear not the path,
   Dark, untrodden, before thee;
Arise and be strong
   For thy God and His glory.

THE TWO SHADOWS.

"The Lord God prepared a gourd, and made it to come up over Jonah, that it might be a shadow over his head, to deliver him from his grief. . . . But God prepared a worm when the morning rose the next day, and it smote the gourd that it withered."—*Jonah* iv. 6, 7.

"A Man shall be as an hiding place from the wind, and a covert from the tempest; as rivers of water in a dry place, as the shadow of a great rock in a weary land."—*Isaiah* xxxii. 2.

"I sat down under His shadow with great delight, and His fruit was sweet to my taste."—*Sol. Song* ii. 3.

LORD, hide me in Thy shadow
   From the east wind's withering blast,
In the secret of Thy presence,
   Till the fervid noon be past.
A worm destroyed the shelter
   Of the gourd Thou gavest me;
My heart is sick and drooping,
   And the sun beats piteously.

Take me, oh, take me to Thee,
   Thou Comforter divine!
My fevered hands—quick! clasp them
   In that pierced palm of Thine.
My drooping head, Lord, shelter
   Upon Thy loving breast;
Thy presence must go with me—
   Wilt Thou not give me rest?

I sat me in the desert
    That dreary day alone,
Counting life's cherished promise
    Of bud and beauty gone.
In my spirit's deep recesses
    A still small voice I heard—
"Better for thee, beloved,
    The withering of thy gourd.

"My hand in love bestowed it,
    To cheer thy desert way;
I will not let My blessing
    Thy trusting heart betray.
Behold, the bower I build thee
    No east wind e'er can blight;
My wings shall be thy shadow;
    My love thy soul's delight.

"It was My hand, beloved one,
    That trained thy sheltering gourd;
The sun scorched at My bidding,
    The wind obeyed My word.
'Twas I prepared in secret
    The worm thou couldst not see,
To bear thy Master's message
    In tenderness to thee.

"Peace, peace! I know thy sorrows,
    Thy faithfulness I prove;
My hand hath weighed thy losses
    In the balance of my love.
Cast down, but not forsaken,
    Despair not, though distrest:
My presence hath been with thee,
    And I will give thee rest.

"Behold a Plant whose beauty
    No scorching breath hath fanned!
A great Rock casts its shadow
    In this dry and thirsty land:
That Rock endures for ever
    The shock of storm and wave;
And the Branch of thy green bower
    Rose from a garden grave."

Ear could not hear the answer
    To my low smothered moan;
Eye hath not seen the rapture
    Beheld by One alone.
A shadow, in that noontide,
    Deeper and deeper grew;
Like healing balm the whisper
    Fell on my heart like dew.

Oh, peace! oh, joy eternal!
  Oh, Love divine and true!
Oh, bloom and fruit immortal
  That Paradise ne'er knew!
Dearer the dreariest desert
  Than all earth's joys restored,
For brighter is Thy presence
  By the withering of my gourd.

THE VOICE IN THE CLOUD.

"The people therefore, that stood by, and heard it, said that it thundered: others said, An angel spake to Him."
John xii. 29.

THE freed bird from its cage hath fled,
  No bond its wings could bind;
It heard a voice within the cloud,
  The cloud with glory lined.

The sound seemed thunder to our hearts,
  The tenderest cords to break;
Our loved one looked beyond the cloud,
  And heard his Father speak.

Sweet singing bird! the darkness hides
  Our minstrel from our eyes;
But thy glad song of triumph now
  Is swelling in the skies.

We would be still; we would rejoice,
  Though vacant is thy place:
The child, within his Father's home,
  Beholds his Father's face.

Thou know'st the rest, that for awhile
  We yet must wait to share;
We praise our God for love to thee,
  While we our burden bear.

We sow the seed in patient hope;
  Soon will the reapers come,
And Christ, returning with His saints,
  Shall bring the harvest home.

I look for Him, our coming Lord;
  My soul no longer grieves:
Soon I shall hear thy song, sweet bird,
  Among the harvest sheaves.

"FEAR NOT."

"Even the very hairs of your head are all numbered. Fear
not therefore: ye are of more value than many sparrows."
Luke xii. 7.

F this Thy promise, gracious Lord,
   Why should I careful be?
I take my staff, Thy faithful Word,
   And cast my care on Thee.

Uphold me, lest I turn aside;
   Sustain me by Thy grace;
And keep me close to Thy dear side,
   The child's appointed place.

If not a hair of mine can fall
   Without my Lord's decree,
Henceforward let me trust for all
   That bows and burdens me.

"O ye of little faith," that God
   Who walked the ocean wild,
Stills the rough waters that He trod,
   And guides His trembling child.

Then why the eye of faith so dim,
   When Christ each cross will bear?
For life or death trust all to Him
   Who numbers every hair.

THE LITTLE SANCTUARY.

"Although I have scattered them among the countries, yet will I be to them as a little sanctuary in the countries where they shall come."—*Ezekiel* xi. 16.

THOU hast been Home and Friend in deserts lonely,
    And Thou wilt be again.
Oh, let me seek Thy smile, my Jesus only,
    And not the praise of men.

Lord, let me feel that Thou art ever nigh me,
    And ruling all in love;
That no good thing Thy wisdom will deny me,
    Thy tenderness to prove.

Thy blessed voice the stormy wind obeyeth,
    And Thy behest fulfils;
Thy word the tempest wild within allayeth,
    And each foreboding stills.

Keep me still close to Thee, O Lord; Thou knowest
    Thou art my hope and rest;
And trustful let me tread the path Thou showest,
    Still leaning on Thy breast.

PROSPERITY.

"I, even I, have spoken; yea, I have called him: I have brought him, and he shall make his way prosperous."
Isaiah xlviii. 15.
"Unto you it is given in the behalf of Christ, not only to believe on Him, but also to suffer for His sake."—*Phil.* i. 29.

IF only in life's pleasant ways
   The Shepherd's tender love is known,
Then may I ask, in sad amaze,
   If still He careth for His own!

But grief, and weariness, and pain,
   Mark where the Man of Sorrows trod;
And he who would the kingdom gain
   Must follow Thee, Thou Son of God.

If days of ease, and nights of rest,
   And sweet affection's gentle bands,
Could woo the wanderer to Thy breast,
   Then might I claim them at Thine hands.

For Thou hast every blessing bought,
   Sealed by Thy piercèd hands above,
And my salvation fully wrought
   From the deep fountain of Thy love.

And yet I ask for prosperous days;
　Nor wilt Thou, Lord, my suit deny:
For while upon Thyself I gaze,
　My soul shall know prosperity.

LOVE'S QUESTION.

"*What I do thou knowest not now; but thou shalt know hereafter.*"—*John* xiii. 7.

"LOVEST thou Me?"
　Ah, Lord, Thou knowest
Each pulse in this cold heart of mine;
　Not in my love I dare to boast,
But I can glory, Lord, in Thine.

Thou lovest me!
　Ah, sweet assurance,
A cross Thou gav'st Thy love to show;
　Lord! let me learn Thy meek endurance,
That I love's height and depth may know.

"Lovest thou Me?"
　Soon I shall know Thee,
Beholding what I see in part;
　Then shall I learn the debt I owe Thee,
And love Thee with unchanging heart.

ONLY A SLING AND STONE.

"Not by might, nor by power, but by my Spirit, saith the Lord of hosts."—Zech. iv. 6.

SAID, "Where shall I flee?
My foes encompass me.
Lord, keep me at Thy side:
There may Thy weakest hide."
But His dear voice replied—

"Fly not! I am thy Shield.
Thou shalt not shrink nor yield,
Nor might nor prowess own;
Take thou thy sling and stone,
Trust in thy God alone."

"Lord, I am but a child,
So easily beguiled,
So swiftly overthrown,"
I answered with a moan;
"I cannot go alone."

"Say not, 'I am a child!'"
And then He sweetly smiled,
And every fear was gone;
"Take thou thy sling and stone;
Thou shalt not go alone!

"Thine eye shall be on Mine,
 My hand upholding thine;
 Though every friend were gone,
 Behold thy faithful One;
 Child, take thy sling and stone!

"Believe, and thou shalt see
 My arm supporting thee;
 My shield is o'er thee thrown,
 Thou hast its shelter known;
 Take now thy sling and stone."

I listened, and drew near;
 Beneath the scorner's sneer
 I heard the mocker's tone—
"Not thus are battles won
 By one weak child alone."

Ah! then I marked it well:
 The giant reeled and fell
 Beneath my sling and stone,
 As I stood there alone;
 But a bright smile on me shone.

Come scorn, come grief, come pain,
 Let me not doubt again;
 I have not stronger grown,
 Nor warfare have I known—
 Only my sling and stone.

JUDAH'S STANDARD.

"On the east side toward the rising of the sun shall they of the standard of the camp of Judah pitch throughout their armies."—*Num.* ii. 3.

THOU, who hast my sins forgiven,
    Shalt my priceless portion be;
In the desert where I wander,
    All my song shall be of Thee.

None beside my soul desireth,
    Though my heart and flesh may fail;
One sweet hope Thy love inspireth,
    Thy compassions cannot fail.

Through the waters round me rolling,
    Safe the pathway Thou hast made;
Thou, the furnace-fire controlling,
    Proved the Rock my sheltering shade.

Keep Thy rescued one beside Thee,
    If I wander yet awhile;
Light the sorrows that betide me
    With a Saviour's loving smile.

Watching for the dawn of morning,
    Oft with desert journeying spent;
Footsore, with my eyes still turning
    To the sunrise from my tent;

I await Thy sweet "Come hither!"
When my week-days' work is done;
Or the golden clouds shall gather,
For the Sabbath morn begun.

THE STRONG REFUGE.

"Christ hath redeemed us from the curse of the law, being made a curse for us: for it is written, Cursed is every one that hangeth on a tree."—*Gal.* iii. 13.

ON to the Refuge!—straight it lies before you;
A Friend is at the door.
Hear, and believe, and live. He tarries for you
As none e'er watched before.
Look to the cross, and there behold Him dying
Upon the accursed tree—
The Lamb of God, in bitter anguish sighing,
Bearing thy sin for thee!

Behold, His precious blood runs freely down;
His sinless head is bowed—
Mocked by the purple robe, the reed, the crown,
Hark to the cruel crowd—
"Let Him come down and save Himself!" Ah me,
Poor soul! what were thy loss
If God's dear Son had saved Himself, not thee,
Upon the murderous cross!

"THE EXCEEDING RICHES OF HIS GRACE."

"They shall see His face; and His name shall be in their foreheads."—Rev. xxii. 4.

SHALL I see my risen Saviour?
   Hear His voice, behold Him nigh?
Touch that very hand extended
   On the cross on Calvary?

Oft my soul seemed nigh to meet Him,
   But death's shadow passed away;
So she folds her wings, awaiting
   For the fair Sabbatic day,

When I never more shall wander,
   Never miss His blessed smile.
Peace, my heart, and trust Him fully
   For the rest this little while!

Sighs have dulled my song's glad measure,
   Sorrows passed with passing days;
But the conflict and the triumph
   Swell the themes of endless praise.

Patience! Let me wait His coming;
   He will share my desert road;
He will keep the soul He purchased
   With the ransom of His blood.

Though so bright, so blest, so beauteous,
    Doth my heavenly mansion shine,
Something fairer, something dearer,
    There I look to claim as mine.

Oh, it is Thyself, Lord Jesus!
    For the richest Gift above
All the gifts art Thou, sweet Giver,
    Who hast crowned me with Thy love.

Grace He'll grant, and I shall need it
    When before His throne I come,
Hear His voice, that quelled the tempest,
    Bid His weary wanderer home.

I shall see His face that sorrowed
    O'er His faithless friends, and trace
Smiles that beamed upon the children
    Folded in His fond embrace.

I shall know the way He led me
    Through the flame and through the flood,
And on many an unseen blessing,
    Read the record, "Asked of God."

There the prayer that seemed rejected,
    And the answer long forgot,
Will await me in the temple,
    Though on earth I knew them not.

Like the storms and clouds of morning,
   In the sunset's radiant glow,
Gathering hues of wondrous beauty,
   For the Lord's resplendent bow.

Grace He grants for joy and sorrow,
   Grace for dying days; and when
I behold my Lord in glory,
   Grace must still my heart sustain.

I shall fall like John before Him,
   With that rapturous sight opprest;
He will stoop in love to raise me
   To the shelter of His breast.

Grace hath found me, grace upholds me,
   Grace will grant me all I need;
Grace secures me Christ and glory—
   This is grace for me indeed!

A beloved servant of the Lord, now gone from our midst, was overheard repeating softly to himself, "I shall have grace even for that." His brother, supposing that he was meditating on the near approach of release from his sufferings, quoted the twenty-third Psalm. "Oh," replied the happy saint cheerfully, "I was not thinking of death, but of seeing the Lord Jesus! I shall gaze in His face, and then I shall fall at His feet, and He will stoop and raise me to His breast; and I shall have grace even for that."

THE WATCH-TOWER.

"Let me not be ashamed; for I put my trust in Thee."
Psalm xxv. 20.
"Thou shalt know that I am the Lord: for they shall not be ashamed that wait for Me."—*Isaiah* xlix. 23.
"It will surely come, it will not tarry."—*Habakkuk* ii. 3.

WILL stand alone on my watch-tower,
   And hear what my Lord will say;
I've watched there many a midnight,
   And the noon of the sultry day.
I have cast my bread on the waters;
   I shall surely find it again,
Though now to my poor heart's vision,
   It seems to be all in vain.

The Lord hath His time appointed;
   I know not when it may be;
But the blessing my soul is seeking
   Will be given at last to me.
It may come in the silent watches,
   When the world lieth weary and still;
It may come when my hope sinks lowest,
   The depth of my spirit to thrill.

I know it will come.   I am gazing
    Into the distance afar,
As the wise men watched for the rising,
    Through Eastern night, of *their* star:
And a Star will rise on *my* darkness
    That Herod shall ne'er destroy;
I shall know the light I have longed for,
    And "rejoice with exceeding joy."

It may come in another fashion
    Than e'er I pictured its ray;
It may rise o'er the dull, cold mountain,
    Like the dawn of a summer's day.
It may come like the lightning flashing,
    Or loud as the thunder's blast;
But the Lord, who is strong in battle,
    Will answer my prayer at last.

Thou hast spoken, and Thou wilt do it:
    I will tarry in hope, and see;
For none ever walked in darkness,
    And waited in vain for Thee.
I know that my prayer will be answered;
    The Lord never comes too late;
And the heart that will trust Him fully
    Shall never be desolate.

It may come when my dust lies sleeping,
    Awaiting my Saviour's call;
But my last prayer, safe in His keeping,
    Will shine there fairest of all.
It may come when the enemy scoffeth,
    But I will believe Thee, Lord;
For they who dwell in Thy presence,
    May take their rest on Thy word.

My star—nay, *Thy* star, my Master!—
    To shine in Thy crown so fair:
This is my hope in my sadness,
    This is the strength of my prayer.
Thou workest in signs and wonders;
    Thy promise shall cheer me again.
Long have I waited on Thee, Lord;
    None ever waited in vain.

I will stand alone on my watch-tower,
    If so I may do Thy will:
Keep me to watch for my star-rise,
    Patiently watching there still.
Thou wilt answer my prayer for Thy glory,
    O Master beloved! Thou wilt bless,
And quicken my heart in Thy praises,
    To tell of Thy faithfulness.

"Therefore I will look unto the Lord; I will wait for the God of my salvation: my God will hear me."—*Micah* vii. 7.

THE WANDERER.

"What is thy Beloved more than another beloved, that thou dost so charge us?"—*Sol. Song* v. 9.

AW ye my soul's Beloved,
    The faithful and the true?
Tell Him I seek Him, sighing,
    Longing to see Him too.

Tell Him, oh, tell Him for me,
    His steps I cannot trace;
I pine till He restore me
    The sunshine of His face.

Who is thy soul's Beloved?
    And whither is He gone?
Why charge us thus? We know not
    Thy lost beloved One.

My Love is white and ruddy:
    Who can His charms declare?
The chief among ten thousand,
    And altogether fair.

I slumbered in the garden,
 I wandered from the way;
I lost the light that led me,
 My joy has passed away.

*   *   *   *   *

I sought Him in the broad way,
 In the city's streets in vain;
Returning to the valley,
 I found my Love again.

"LIGHT SOWN FOR THE RIGHTEOUS."

"Until the time that His word came: the word of the Lord tried him."—*Psalm* cv. 19.

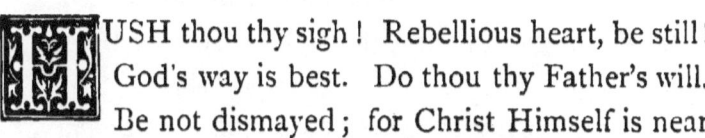USH thou thy sigh! Rebellious heart, be still!
God's way is best. Do thou thy Father's will.
Be not dismayed; for Christ Himself is near
This "doleful way!" Unto His listening ear
Pour out thy broken plaint, and soon, how soon,
The wail of woe will change to joy's sweet tune!
A little while, and then shall pass away
The veil that shrouds His beauty, and the day
Dawn in the cloudless morning ne'er to cease;
For light is sown for thee, and joy and peace
Laid up for those who love the Father's will.
Peace, troubled heart! Hush, murmuring lips! Be still!

THE LOST CHERITH.

"He drank of the brook. And it came to pass after a while, that the brook dried up."—1 *Kings* xvii. 6, 7.

THOU hast but claimed Thine own; Lord, I surrender
    Thy precious loan, for I would do Thy will;
Let me not doubt Thy love so true and tender,
    Say to my quivering heart-strings, " Peace, be still."

Christ! Priest and King! In yon bright realm of glory
    Thou bear'st a brother's sympathy for woe;
And 'mid the songs of seraphs rise before Thee
    The broken prayers—the sighs I breathe below.

Thou heard'st my cry when sore athirst and weary,
    And on my path in pity cast Thine eyes;
Then in the arid waste, all parched and dreary,
    Thou bad'st for me a bubbling streamlet rise.

"Drink," Lord, Thou saidst: and I in mute thanksgiving
    Drank of the stream that by the wayside burst,
Sweet drops of love from Thy deep fount upspringing,
    That soothed my weariness and quenched my thirst.

Now at Thy word dries up my pleasant Cherith,
   Oh let me not in selfish grief repine;
Only Thy voice my mourning spirit heareth,
   Thou hast not taken mine, O Lord, but *Thine.*

" Nay, *thine* and *Mine!*" (thus came a whisper stealing
   On my sad heart, and tenderly it fell;)
" That spring of joy I sent, my love revealing,
   And its deep secret, thou must ponder well.

"'Tis Mine and thine: it was my love that lent it,
   Thy lonely pilgrim path to wander by;
Fear not, my child, it was thy Father sent it,
   And the same love now bids the brook run dry.

" Thy song of praise that with its murmurs blended,
   Rejoiced His heart who trod the earth *alone,*
Thy stifled wail 'mid angel hosts ascended,
   And reached thy Brother on thy Father's throne.

" The cistern fails—the fountain flows for ever;
   Child, to *My* care thy dearest ones resign;
My arms uphold thee, I will leave thee never,
   And all I am, and all I have, is thine!"

Lord! Friend and Brother! safe with Thee be treasured
   Memories of countless mercies past recall;
Thy lovingkindness is not scant or measured,
   Thou art Thyself the first best gift of all.

O Christ! Thou art my fountain ever flowing,
  Love passing knowledge, knowing no decline;
All, all is love in taking or bestowing,
  And my sweet wayside brook is Thine and mine!

INCARNATE LOVE.

"Having loved His own which were in the world, He loved them unto the end."—John xiii. 1.

UP, mourning soul! though shadows round thee hover;
  Up to the stronghold! Christ's own might is thine.
Doth danger threaten? Lo! His wings shall cover,
  And thou shalt say, "Behold, His strength is mine!"
In the sweet radiance of His presence sun thee,
  When faithless hearts and harsh words wound thee sore;
Lean on that loving breast whose blood hath won thee
  The right to rest there now—and evermore.

THE PRISONER OF THE LORD.

"This is the work of God, that ye believe on Him whom
He hath sent."—*John* vi. 29.
"The Lord thy God hath given thee rest."—*Deut.* xxv. 19.

LORD, I would work for Thee,
   In Thy wide field afar;
The joyful song wakes echoes sweet
   Where Thy dear servants are.
Vain seems my life for Thee,
   While I sit here apart;
Oh, give to me the hearing ear
   And understanding heart!

"My child, yon busy scene
   Is not assigned to thee;
Thou hast a place upon the Rock—
   There thou shalt rest with Me.
The pine-tree loves the plain,
   The cedar seeks the height,
But myrtles in the valley low
   May bear their blossoms white.

"Is it so hard a lot—
   This stillness and this rest—
To suffer with Me for awhile,
   And be for ever blest;

To know My hand of love
    Upholding in the gloom,
That not a cloud too dark should break
    To mar My myrtle's bloom?

"Safe from the scorching day
    Thy sheltered life hath been,
The storms that swept above the hill
    Have left My valleys green.
Life's deep mysterious scroll
    A sealèd book must be;
The service of thy Father's house
    Is to believe on Me.

"Within My dwelling-place
    Thy tender life shall hide;
Enough that I have need of thee—
    Only with Me abide."
Lord, teach me as Thou wilt
    The mysteries of Thy grace;
Content, if only I may share
    The sunshine of Thy face.

FAITH'S VENTURE.

"Buy thee my field that is in Anathoth: for the right of redemption is thine to buy it. . . . Behold, I am the Lord, the God of all flesh: is there any thing too hard for Me?"
Jer. xxxii. 7, 27.

OH, buy the field, the priceless field,
    And lay thy silver down;
A thousandfold the land shall yield—
    A kingdom and a crown.

Fear not, though many a mighty foe
    Against thy walls advance;
Jehovah's arm will lay them low
    For thy deliverance.

Oh, take Him at His royal word,
    That word that cannot lie;
Thy shield and sword is Israel's Lord—
    Almighty sovereignty!

Believe His love, who holds the land,
    Oh trust in Him alone;
And claim His promise from the hand
    Of Christ, the Righteous One.

Delivered once from Egypt's chain,
  Led through the pathless wave;
And by a thousand ways again
  He proves His power to save.

Then forward, soul! though all is dim
  To nature's bounded sense;
Thy every need is known to Him
  Whose strength's—Omnipotence!

THE TWO FOUNTAINS.

"What meanest thou, O sleeper? arise, call upon thy God."
Jonah i. 6.

OH, tarry not, and look not thou behind thee!
    Sleeper, arise;
  The past in iron fetters will but bind thee,
    And cloud thine eyes;
For the world proffers but the fleeting dreams
    Thou know'st too well,
False with the serpent's wiles whose beauty gleams
    With light from hell.

Closed is the gate, and seraphs watch the garden
    Whence sprang our woes,
And o'er the threshold, past the angel warden,
    A fountain flows—

A stream of bitter water, ceasing never
    Through these long years,
Still wandering onward to dark Jordan's river,
    The fount of tears.

There is another fountain softly flowing,
    It springs above;
Hope, life, and peace, and joy, that spring bestowing,
    From God's deep love.
Open for thee, the smitten Rock is pouring
    The living wave,
Healing the broken heart, and oft restoring
    The life it gave.

It was for *thee* the Holy One was smitten,
    For thy great need;
It was for *thee* the Word of Life was written,
    Then rise and read;
And in the light the wondrous page unfolding,
    Like one of old,
Thou wilt exclaim, our King's rich store beholding,
    "Not half was told."

EBENEZER.

"Take heed to thyself, and keep thy soul diligently, lest thou forget the things which thine eyes have seen, and lest they depart from thy heart."—*Deut.* iv. 9.

ARE the burdens that press thee thus sorely
    Too heavy for Jesus to lighten?
Are the clouds that o'ershadow thy pathway
    Too dark for the Spirit to brighten?

Believe in His love, and remember
    The way thy Redeemer hath brought thee;
Thou hast passed the wild desert; forget not
    The lessons of love He hath taught thee.

Look back on the mountain thou traversed,
    When the pathway seems rugged before thee,
And know whose the Hand leading on
    To the home of thy rest and His glory.

Let the worldling despise thee and leave thee;
    He knows not the joy of thy sorrow;
The Friend who has loved thee and led thee
    Will lead thee and love thee to-morrow.

Each day is a step drawing nearer
    To the rest that remaineth for ever;
And thy sorrows shall swell to a pæon,
    And echo beyond the dark river.

IN AND OUT.

"I am the door: by Me if any man enter in, he shall be saved, and shall go in and out, and find pasture."—*John* x. 9.

LORD, in Thy presence let me hide,
I ask for nothing else beside;
In for my food and rest, and then
Forth to proclaim Thy love again;
Still sheltered by Thy hand, O Lord,
Still listening for Thy whispered word!

Thy empty vessel silent lies,
Still waiting for its fresh supplies;
Some long-sought blessing to obtain,
And prove I waited not in vain
To brace my heart, and so proclaim
The shelter of Jehovah's Name.

How oft have faithless fears assailed!
The cruse of oil has almost failed.
The meal was low, and hope the same,
When He, long looked for, surely came;
And I began to praise anew
My God, the faithful and the true.

THE STONE ROLLED AWAY.

"Be not affrighted: Ye seek Jesus of Nazareth, which was crucified."—*Mark* xvi. 6.

SAD is my heart, and dark as cold;
   No light, no joy, is mine:
Return, Thou Holy Comforter,
   With hope and peace divine!

Oh, let Thy soft reviving beams
   Show Christ alone my trust,
Although my faithless spirit seems
   Still cleaving to the dust!

Earth holds no light for me, O Lord!
   Since I Thy face have seen;
I hear no whisper in Thy Word,
   The thunder rolls between.

O Holy Comforter! restore
   The only joy I crave;
O Lord! reveal Thyself once more;
   By Thy salvation—save!

*   *   *   *   *

I hear the words of tenderness,
   Sealed with my Saviour's blood:
"I will not leave thee comfortless;
   Behold the Lamb of God!"

A PLEA FOR THE PROMISE.

"Sanctify them through Thy truth: Thy word is truth."
John xvii. 17.

MY plea is not my love, Lord;
   For that is cold and faint.
My plea is not my work, Lord;
   For that is poor and scant.
Father, I urge my only plea—
   Christ's love to me.

I hold Thy Word, Thine own Word;
   'Tis all that I can bring.
I claim Thy faithful promise, Lord,
   As to Thy cross I cling;
And through my blinding tears I see
   Thy love to me.

Past human comprehension,
   Oh, mighty, wondrous grace!
Among His blood-bought trophies
   He finds for me a place.
And evermore my song shall be,
   Christ's love to me.

I wandered far from Thee, Lord,
    And I was sore afraid;
I feared to hear Thy voice, Lord,
    'Twas sin the shadow made.
But in Thy light I only see
    Thy love to me.

Teach me to trace Thy hand, Lord,
    My eyes are backward cast;
And I can trust my future
    From all the wondrous past.
Above, around, I only see
    Thy love to me.

THE HAVEN GAINED.

"It is the Lord: let Him do what seemeth Him good."
1 *Sam.* iii. 18.

I SAW a taper's light
    Wane 'neath the wild wind's sigh;
The twilight faded into night,
    And a new star shone on high.

A little lamp of love
    Sinks 'neath love's fondest care:
Look in the temple's court above,
    Christ hath removed it there.

I saw a tiny bark
  Float o'er a summer sea
With snow-white sail, and pennon dark;
  Strange seemed the sight to me.

No foot was on the prow,
  No living freight it bore;
Swift as the light it seemed to go,
  Away to the shadowy shore.

Blue was the sky o'erhead,
  Bright was the wave beneath;
The glistening sail its white folds spread:
  My soul felt the chill of death.

* * * *

What ails thee, child? For, hark!
  A murmured cry is heard;
A little soul, in the spirit-bark,
  Hath fled like an ocean bird.

Thou hast early found thy rest:
  Peace to thee! fair white dove;
Thou art folded safe on thy Saviour's breast,
  In the arms of Eternal Love.

THE NEW AND LIVING WAY.

"That I may know Him, and the power of His resurrection, and the fellowship of His sufferings, being made conformable unto His death."—Phil. iii. 10.

LORD! I fain would love Thee more,
    Learn Thy precepts, do Thy will,
Seek Thy dealings to adore,
    Trust Thy wisdom, and be still.

I believe Thy love to me,
    Seen in all Thy wondrous ways:
Shall my heart as marble be,
    Cold and silent in Thy praise?

Oft I say, "For me He died,"
    Yet my sinking spirit grieves;
Let my foes in darkness hide,
    For I know my Saviour lives.

Lives His weakest one to bless;
    Lives! the burden of my song;
Lives! a fount of blessedness;
    Lives! to love me all day long!

Once I mourned my thorny road,
    Once I wept my weary feet;
Now He takes my lightest load,
    And He makes my service sweet.

Lo! the Hand I pierced, I see,
    Opens wide my Father's door;
And on high to plead for me,
    Jesus lives for evermore.

THE INVITATION.

"But one thing is needful."—*Luke* x. 42.

COME, ye toiling hearts that labour,
    Here the mourner findeth rest;
And like John, beloved, and loving,
    Lean on Jesus' tender breast.

Drink new draughts of consolation;
    Draw new strength and fresh supplies
From that pure heart's deathless fountain,
    Whence eternal pleasures rise.

Fly not to the gloomy covert,
    With the wound the archers gave;
Seek the smile of love to heal thee;
    Sin hath smitten—Christ can save.

See! He waiteth to receive thee;
    Come, thou soul with grief opprest;
Weary ones and heavy laden,
    Come, and Christ will give you rest.

SOWING IN HOPE.

"But some man will say, How are the dead raised up? and with what body do they come? . . . That which thou sowest, thou sowest not that body that shall be : . . . but God giveth it a body as it hath pleased Him."—1 *Cor.* xv. 35, 37, 38.

WE laid our darling in the dust,
    And homeward bent our feet,
    Until the rising of the just,
    When we again shall meet.
We laid her 'mid the fading flowers;
    But, fairer far than they,
    She winged her flight
    To realms of light,
    And everlasting day.

We laid her down with many a tear;
    She was so young, so fair!
    But now we weep not o'er the dust,
    We know she is not there.
Faith beckons where our darling dwells.
    Jesus, we look to see
    Eternal spring,
    When Thou shalt bring
    Our blossom back with Thee.

THE LIVING GOD.

"Fear not; I am the first and the last: I am He that liveth, and was dead; and, behold, I am alive for evermore, Amen; and have the keys of hell and of death."
Rev. i. 17, 18.

GOD lives! Then why should I despond,
  As if no help were near?
He knows the sorrows of my heart;
  He chose my portion here:
Therefore my grief to Him I bring,
And tell my Saviour everything.

PSALM xxxiv. 15.

God sees! I cannot weep unseen;
  Then why do I complain?
He numbers every tear; He knows
  The cause of all my pain:
He looks upon my misery,
And He will surely comfort me.

ISAIAH lxv. 24.

God hears, though listen none beside!
  Then wherefore do I fear?
As if my cry could fail to reach
  My God's attentive ear:

"Amen" with my petition blends,
And swift deliverance He sends.

Isaiah xlii. 16.

God leads! Then, O my soul, thy path
    In patient hope pursue!
The world lays snares around my feet,
    But Christ will guard me through:
And though mysteriously He guide,
My hand in His, I cannot slide.

Luke xi. 13.

God gives! Then why, my soul, so poor?
    And thy provision scant?
When God the Giver is so rich,
    Why dost thou pine in want?
Though in a desert land I be,
My Shepherd can provide for me.

1 Thess. v. 24.

God lives! Behold Him everywhere.
    God hears! Then call for aid.
God sees, and numbers every tear!
    God leads! Be not afraid.
God lives and loves; and grace He'll give,
That thou eternally with Him mayst live!

From the German.

"HE SAITH."

"Thou hast dealt well with Thy servant, O Lord, according unto Thy word. . . . I rejoice at Thy word, as one that findeth great spoil."—*Psalm* cxix. 65, 162.

WHEN the Father His little one smiteth,
 A blessing must brood underneath;
I will walk by the lamp that He lighteth,
 And rest on the word that "He saith."

He saith, "I will never forsake thee,"
 Each day He proclaims it anew;
And again to my Rock I betake me,
 And prove that His promise is true.

He saith, "I will guide thee:" oh, never
 Distrust the full truth of His word;
To-day, and to-morrow—for ever,
 Let me rest on Thy promise, my Lord.

I know He is faithful who said it,
 'Tis written and sealed in His word;
And day after day I have read it,
 And said, "I believe Thee, my Lord."

But do I believe it and live it,
   And know He is willing to be
As true as His word, and to give it
   A thousand times better to me?

A mansion is mine, He'll prepare it,
   Though the least of His servants am I;
And, better than all, He will share it,
   As ages on ages go by.

When I gaze on the wild roaring billow,
   Shall I fear He will leave me alone?
Reposing no more on a pillow,
   He watches His child from the Throne.

And yet, when the storm riseth higher,
   And again on the waves I am tost,
I forget that my Saviour is nigher,
   And cry in despair, "I am lost!"

He saith, "Call, and I will deliver,"
   He hath won me from sin and from death;
Shall I dread, then, the dark rolling river,
   When I hope in the word that He saith?

When the terrors of death shall assail me,
   Shall I cling to a cistern of clay?
Shall I rest on a reed that will fail me,
   When Jehovah's right hand is my stay?

Is the Saviour unwilling to give us
  The riches He rose to bestow?
Will the God of our mercies deceive us?
  No! Calvary's cross answers No!

How poor are earth's richest resources,
  How rich is each promise to me;
Though some trust in chariots and horses,
  Lord, let me trust only in Thee.

THE LAST JOURNEY.

"They two went on."— 2 *Kings* ii. 6.

SO far with me, no farther now,
  Our journey all so brief is done;
Thou goest on thine unseen way,
  And I must tread my path alone.

"They two went on," and we have been
  Through Bethel's plain and Jordan's flood;
Then one went back to serve and wait,
  And one soared up to dwell with God.

We two went on. Ah! not alone;
  And though no car of light I see,
There walks with me the Holy One,—
  And Christ the Living God with thee.

THE STRONGHOLD.

"O Lord, Thou art my God; I will exalt Thee, I will praise Thy name; for Thou hast done wonderful things; Thy counsels of old are faithfulness and truth."—*Isaiah* xxv. 1.

LORD, my God, by Thee
   My lonely path is made!
Why do I shun Thy cross?
   Why am I thus afraid?
The storm may howl in wrath,
   And clouds obscure the light:
Thou guidest still my path;
   'Tis ever in Thy sight.

Before me Thou wilt go:
   Thou keepest watch above;
Thou know'st the way I do not know,
   And all Thy ways are love.
O Thou sweet Dove of Peace!
   My sinking spirit fill;
Show me, though comforts cease,
   That Thou art with me still.

Thou art my strength, O Lord!
   And when, with grief opprest,
I trust Thy faithful word,
   My stronghold and my rest!

My hiding-place I find,
My shadow from the heat,
My shelter from the desert wind—
All, all at Jesus' feet.

WATCH!

"Be sober, be vigilant; because your adversary the devil, as a roaring lion, walketh about, seeking whom he may devour: whom resist stedfast in the faith."—1 *Peter* v. 8, 9.

KEEP thy watch, it is daybreak,
　Though all seems misty now;
Watch, for a star will guide thee
　Afar o'er the mountain brow.
Mean unto men the treasures
　Thy labour of love will bring;
But better than gold and jewels
　To the heart of thy heavenly King.

Keep thy watch in the morning,
　Though the sky seems bright and clear;
A cloud in the west is rising,
　A tempest is hovering near.
Thou say'st it is nought, but watch it,
　Thou knowest not what it may be;
If thine ears are open to hear it,
　It bringeth a message to thee.

Keep thy watch at the noontide,
　In the warmth of its fervid glow;
Thou art lost in thy vineyard labour,
　But a serpent may hide below.
A lion lurks in the thicket,
　Thou say'st he is sleeping or dead;
But he waiteth for careless footsteps,
　And marketh the path that they tread.

Keep thy watch in the evening,
　When the labour of day is done,
For many a poisonous vapour
　Will rise with the setting sun.
But watch, for thy Lord is near thee,
　As when in the fruitful field,
And lean on the love that leads thee:
　He is thy Sun and thy Shield.

Keep thy watch at the midnight,
　Mark the stars as they rise;
Listen, and they will tell thee
　How sure are His promises.
True was His care in the morning,
　Safe is the truth of His word:
Thy Sun and thy Shield in the noontide
　Is at even thy great Reward.

LIGHT AND SHADOW.

"Who knoweth not in all these that the hand of the Lord hath wrought this?"—Job xii. 9.

SEE where the sunlight falls
   In its golden glow;
Soft through the olive boughs
   Shadows come and go.
God bade the lily bloom,
   And the thunder roll;
Each hath a voice from Him
   To the list'ning soul.

Take thou the cloud from Him,
   Take thou the light;
Day brings the eventide,
   Eventide the night.
All hath a word from Him—
   Child, listen well,
Learn why the sunlight failed,
   When the shadow fell.

THE SOUL'S PETITION.

"Ask, and it shall be given you."—*Matt.* vii. 7.

OH for a priceless crown of stars
    To cast before the Throne,
And a seraph's voice of melody
    To tell what grace hath done;
To sing Thy praise, O Lamb of God,
    Who for the sinner died;
To tell the love of Him once slain—
    Jesus, the Crucified.

Grant me an ear attuned to know
    Each whisper of Thy love,
And in Thy light to shun the snare
    That scares Thine Holy Dove;
And faith, Lord! faith to follow Thee,
    As o'er the waters dark
We seek the shipwrecked mariner,
    Or save the foundering bark.

Grant, Lord, unto this longing heart
    Thy blood hath washed from sin,
To image back Thy holiness,
    As Thou dost dwell within.

Give me a will subdued and meek,
    Obedient to Thy Word,
To prove the might of Him who lives—
    Jesus, my risen Lord.

Give to my hand a heavenly harp,
    To hymn Thy matchless worth,
To echo o'er the sea of glass,
    While waiting still on earth :
Cause it to break the sleeper's dream,
    And downcast spirits cheer;
And to Thy watching people tell,
    The Bridegroom draweth near.

Give, Lord,—I ask it from Thy grace,—
    The heart, the harp, the crown ;
I ask them for Thy service here,
    And all shall be thine own.
I bless Thee for Thy love's sweet seal,
    And nought Thy love can sever ;
Lord, lead me on from faith to faith
    To follow Thee for ever.

THE SWELLING OF JORDAN.

"When ye are come to the brink of the water of Jordan, ye shall stand still in Jordan."—*Joshua* iii. 8.
"As I was with Moses, so I will be with thee: I will not fail thee, nor forsake thee."—*Joshua* i. 5.

BE still, O Jordan's billows!
   And stay thy rushing tide,
Until I stem thy current
   "On to the other side."
My heart with fear is sinking
   As the waters touch my feet;
How shall I tread the pathway
   When the wild waves o'er me meet?

I thought a band of angels
   Would wait to lead me home;
I thought the gates of glory
   Would glisten through the gloom—
That the joyful hymn of seraphs
   Would cheer the starless wave,
And hide death's dismal pageant,
   The death-throe and the grave.

Darker my path is growing;
   I falter on the brink;
If, with my foes contending,
   My trembling soul shall shrink,
Then they who watch my halting
   Before the Jordan's flood
Will cry, "Behold the boaster
   Who anchored on his God."

The rolling river whispers,
   "Where is the vaunted faith
That, in life's summer-morning,
   Unshrinking, looked on death?
You thought to cross the Jordan
   Like the light bark, fair and fleet,
And now you fail and tremble
   When the cold waves kiss your feet.

"Ah, stand still, and remember
   Your unbelief and pride;
Read o'er your life's long record,
   In stains of crimson dyed,
Your Saviour oft forsaken
   And wounded, as you strayed,
Unprized the love that sought you,
   Your Friend and Lord betrayed!"

All true—most true! A sinner
    By pride and passion tossed,
Who had no plea for pardon,
    Ruined, and dead, and lost!
But Jesus, oft forsaken,
    Hath rescued me, I know,
And my sins, as red as scarlet,
    Are now as white as snow.

Then a song rose in the darkness,
    And softly on my sight
A track of golden glory
    Touched every wave with light.
'Twas a Father's sweet compassion,
    Lest my weary soul should sink,
And my foes rejoice above me
    As I stood on Jordan's brink.

"Nay, child, these roaring waters
    Will not be passed alone,
A path is made already,
    Where the living God hath gone;
And He who went before thee
    Is watching o'er thee now;
His hand upholds thee, fainting,
    With the death-dew on thy brow.

"Yea, 'stand still,' and remember
    The way thy steps were led;
His arms (the Everlasting)
    Are ceaselessly outspread;
Not one good thing was lacking,
    And they who watch shall see,
That as I was with Moses,
    So will I be with thee.

"Fear not th' accuser's malice;
    His rage shall be in vain;
And the foes that now surround thee
    Thou ne'er shalt see again.
The Ark hath crossed before thee
    Through Jordan's swelling flood,
And the path through these wild waters
    Is traced with Jesus' blood."

I trust in Thee, Lord Jesus!
    Though darkness veil Thy face;
It cannot dim one promise
    Of faithfulness and grace.
I passed the Red Sea's fury,
    And death I shall not see;
For as Thou wert with Moses,
    So wilt Thou be with me!

I have no song of triumph;
   My lips forget the lay;
My hand forgets her cunning
   On my broken harp to-day.
But Christ is my salvation,
   And all my heart can bring—
The Lamb once slain for sinners,
   My Saviour, Lord, and King!

Glory to Thee for ever,
   Who rulest Jordan's wave;
Glory to Thee, Lord Jesus,
   Who came to seek and save.
I hear amid the swelling
   Of the dark, tempestuous tide,
"Welcome to thee, poor sinner,
   For whom the Saviour died."

THE SECRET DWELLING PLACE.

"He shall cover thee with His feathers, and under His wings shalt Thou trust: His truth shall be thy shield and buckler."—*Psalm* xci. 4.

OH, fierce the foes that never tire,
   And never cease their wrath!
But Thou, Lord, art a wall of fire
   About Thy children's path.

Thou seest the conflict close and sharp
   None others gaze upon,
And angels strike a golden harp
   For every victory won.

At night encamped around our bed
   There waits a shining band;
And where the evil spirits tread,
   God's holy angels stand.

Then, shall I dread the darksome night,
   Or fear the fowler's snare,
When midnight is as noonday bright,
   And Thou art everywhere?

Safe sheltered 'neath Thy canopy,
  I will in danger hide,
The arrows harmless passing by,
  While I with Thee abide.

Cover me, Lord! my trust shall be
  In Thee and Thy great Name;
For he whose hope is set on Thee,
  Thou ne'er hast left to shame.

Then why so troubled, O my soul,
  And why cast down art thou?
He who delivered thee from death
  Is near to save thee now.

He cannot leave thee nor forsake,
  His arms are round thee thrown;
As the mountains fence Jerusalem,
  He compasseth His own.

THROUGH THE LATTICE.

"Whom having not seen, ye love; in whom, though now ye see Him not, yet believing, ye rejoice with joy unspeakable and full of glory."—1 *Peter* i. 8.

UNDER the shadow of thy boughs,
   O fair celestial tree,
I eat the everlasting fruit
   Thy life brings forth for me.
When shall I see Thee, as Thou art?
   My fainting spirit dies,
Failing between the lattice, Lord,
   Thy face to recognise.

Make haste, Beloved! Turn to me
   Till shadows hence depart,
Fly fleetly o'er the spicy hills
   Like some swift-footed hart.
Come! to thy valley-garden, come,
   Swift as the bounding roe;
My longing heart shall hold Thee there,
   And never let Thee go.

GOD'S UNSPEAKABLE GIFT.

"The Father sent the Son to be the Saviour of the world."
1 *John* iv. 14.
"By Him therefore let us offer the sacrifice of praise to God continually, that is, the fruit of our lips giving thanks to His name."—*Hebrews* xiii. 15.

I PRAISE Thee, O my Father,
    For all Thy grace to me,—
Thy arm hath set my captive soul
    From sin's dominion free;
For trust to know Thy faithfulness
    Will keep me to the end:
And, first and last, I thank Thee
    For Christ, the sinner's Friend!

I thank Thee for the Comforter,
    This wandering heart to teach;
For all the heights and depths, O God,
    No finite mind can reach;
For strength, so freely granted me,
    Through countless ages stored:
And, first and last, I thank Thee
    Through Christ, my risen Lord!

I praise Thee for Thy boundless love,
   That gave Thy Son to die,
To bring again Thy banished one
   From sin and misery;
I thank Thee for the victory
   O'er sin and Satan won:
And, first and last, I thank Thee
   For the gift of Thy dear Son!

I thank Thee Thou hast been my light
   On many a pathless plain;
And when I sought Thy presence there,
   I never sought in vain.
Thy hand controls the howling storm,
   Thy foot is on the sea;
How can I tread the waters, Lord,
   Unless I walk with Thee?

Oh it is worth the sharpest cross
   Christ's fellowship to share;
The dearest things shall be as dross
   One pain for Him to bear,
Who bore the curse of sin for me,
   And bowed His head to shame,
That I, from condemnation free,
   Might triumph in His Name.

I praise Thee for the pathway rough—
So much I need Thy care;
I thank Thee for the solace sweet
When only Thou art near!
"Thus will I bless Thee while I live;"
And when my race is run,
I'll praise Thee still, my Father,
For the gift of Thy dear Son!

ABIDING.

"When the Spirit of truth is come, He will guide you into all truth."—John xvi. 13.

CHRIST, the Fountain of my blessing,
Grants the Father's promise still;
Thus I learn my untold riches,
And obey His heavenly will.

Shall I slight the gift and Giver?
Shall I sin my light away?
Nay, come now, O Holy Spirit,
And abide with me to-day.

God of truth and God of promise,
Thou dost undertake to bless;
Dwell in me in full possession,
God of light and holiness.

THE UNKNOWN PATH.

"The vision is yet for an appointed time, but at the end it shall speak, and not lie."—*Hab.* ii. 3.

THERE passed along a weary man,
   Led by a little child,
Whose feeble hand had clasped his own;
   And, looking down, he smiled
At such a messenger, to guide
   His feet along the way
Bestrewn with broken rocks, and hid
   From the sweet light of day.

Sadder became his face, and dark,
   Darker the toilsome road;
The world's roar in the distance seems
   Like some out-bursting flood.
Before them, through an open porch,
   There breaks a silvery beam,
That trembles o'er th' untrodden way
   Like starlight on a stream.

No footstep echoes now! No sound
   In that drear path is heard:
Though many a noiseless traveller passed,
   None spake to them a word.

Vainly the child would cheer the gloom,
    As shadows round them spread,
But every accent died away
    In the silence of the dead.

How cold this cavern seems, how long
    And strange this silent track,
Yet never on the lonely way
    The travellers turned back.
But now they pause, and now they part,
    In that mysterious spot;
"Stand still, O feeble messenger,
    Thy Master needs thee not!

"Stand still! and see a pathway made,
    Where Jesus went before,
For he who walks with thee to-day,
    Ne'er crossed it heretofore."
Gently the childish hand unclasps
    The strong one from its hold,
And points him to the open porch
    Where fairer scenes unfold.

Far, far beyond, like Tabor's hill,
    They mark the mountains rise,
And a sunny shore unveils before
    The watchers' wistful eyes.

Bright glows his face as through the porch
    The traveller is gone;
The child is watching on the way,
    But keeps that watch alone.

There is no room for two to pass
    Where only one hath trod;
Each separate soul that gains the goal
    Must stand alone with God.
The weary man is resting now,
    His rest is deep and sweet;
And the faithful servant's journey ends
    At his dear Master's feet.

THE HOUSE NOT MADE WITH HANDS.

"If I go and prepare a place for you, I will come again, and receive you unto Myself; that where I am, there ye may be also."—*John* xiv. 3.

AR upon a shining shore,
    Where no noisy breakers roar,
    Is my home—for evermore.

    Earth's possessions lost their spell,
    In the joy no tongue can tell,
    When I bade the world farewell.

Rich the portion I shall share,
Fair the mansion! oh, how fair!
For my Father reigneth there.

As the wild waves wander by,
Let me check each rising sigh,
In my heart continually.

For I walk the swelling flood,
Washed in Jesus' precious blood,
And my home—my home with God!

Soul! bend meekly to thy cross,
Counting all earth's gain as loss,
And her fairest treasures dross.

Bright, and yet more clearly, shine
Through the clouds, sweet home of mine.
Then no more shall I repine.

Jesus Christ has gone before,
Christ the Way, the Light, the Door,
Here I rest for evermore!

"AARON'S BREASTPLATE."

"Aaron shall bear their names before the Lord upon his two shoulders for a memorial. . . . Aaron shall bear the names of the children of Israel in the breastplate of judgment upon his heart, when he goeth in unto the holy place, for a memorial before the Lord continually."
Exodus xxviii. 12, 29.
"Christ is not entered into the holy places made with hands, which are the figures of the true; but into heaven itself, now to appear in the presence of God for us."—*Heb.* ix. 24.

IN the wondrous breastplate golden,
Safely on His bosom holden,
  See the jewels from the mine !
Amethyst and onyx, wearing
Mystic marks, and each one bearing
  Traces of the hand divine.

Sapphires 'mid the gorgeous cluster
Sparkle with celestial lustre,
  Like the crystal dome above ;
Ruby rare and topaz blending
In that glory never-ending,
  Safe upon the breast of love.

Emerald and beryl throwing
Chastened hues, the fairer growing
   As the jasper blends the rays;
Chrysopras, like king's attire,
Glowing like a star of fire,
   Or a soul that loves to praise.

Who the love and pain can measure,
Ere revealed this hidden treasure,
   One by one, in dazzling light?
On His breast our High Priest wears them,
On His shoulder, see, He bears them,
   Ever in our Father's sight.

Can one jewel lack its station?
Nay, for through much tribulation
   Christ hath won them for His own.
Veiled on earth, by sorrow faded,
Clouds of care their beauty shaded,—
   But behold them near the Throne!

They in Christ. How fair! how glorious!
Feeble ones in Him victorious,—
   Who that bond of love can sever?
All so fair—not one is fairer,
All so dear—not one is dearer,
   All in Christ,—yea, Christ's for ever!

THE SHINING FOOTPRINT.

"I am the Light of the world : he that followeth Me shall not walk in darkness, but shall have the light of life."
John viii. 12.
"We walk by faith, not by sight."—2 *Cor.* v. 7.

DARK the way I wander:
   Shall I then go back?
   Nay! I trace a footprint
     On the desert track,
   And I hear a whisper
     (Sweeter could not be),
   "Lo, I go before thee,
     Rise! and follow Me."

So I rose up quickly,
   With my staff in hand,
Gath'ring strength in rising
   At my Lord's command;
Yet I thought (half sighing),
   "Not a step I see!"
"On!" He said, "the darkness
   Hideth not from Me."

For awhile I lingered,
  Still on sunshine bent;
Not a ray broke o'er me,
  All the way I went;
But upon the waters
  Seemed that step to be;
O'er the billows whispered,
  "Come and follow Me."

There were thousand footprints
  On my way before,
Free and far they wandered,
  On that sandy shore.
One, unlike all others
  In its lucid light,
Left a path of glory
  Through the gloomy night.

By the stormy waters,
  In the busy street,
Through the dreary alley,
  'Mid the crowding feet,
Gleams that shining footprint,
  All may seek and see;
And the voice of Jesus
  Whispers, "Follow Me."

Lord, keep Thou my footsteps
  Very near to Thine,
That some ray of glory
  On my path may shine;
Nearer and still nearer
  Draw my heart to Thee,
Lest I lose thy whisper—
  "Rise and follow Me."

"HOME OF REST" FOR WEARY WORKERS.

"And I beheld, and, lo, in the midst of the throne and of the four beasts, and in the midst of the elders, stood a Lamb as it had been slain."—*Rev.* v. 6.

IN this home of heavenly mansions,
  Where we look our Lord to meet,
Thoughts e'en now, like holy angels,
  Flit along the golden street.

Light celestial gilds the threshold,
  From the Throne of God within;
And yon gate shuts out for ever
  All the fierce assaults of sin

Safe from tears that leave their traces,
    Far from falsehood and from scorn,
Safe from death and heart-sick partings—
    Oh, that coming cloudless morn!

Hid from snares that track the footsteps,
    From the sneer and mocking smile,
From the wasting noonday sickness,
    From the serpent's treacherous guile.

Over now our days of labour—
    And, in robes of whiteness dressed,
Let us come, and gaze a moment,
    On our future home of rest.

Leave your cares, forget your sorrows,
    Here the eye can ne'er wax dim;
Come in spirit to these mansions,
    Come and rest awhile with Him.

Oh, how fair these fair foundations!
    Oh, how glorious is the sight!
Saints and angels gather round us,
    Basking in the Lamb's pure light.

In those climes of golden summer
    Steals no cloud or racking pain;
Never more comes sin or sadness;
    Fear shall shadow ne'er again.

Thou art there, O God of Glory:
Never, since the world began,
Was a sight like this before me—
Son of God and Son of Man!

Lo, I trace Him in the garden!
Where the midnight watch He keeps;
On the mountain, supplicating
For the world that round Him sleeps.

Bearing all our sin and sorrow,
Bleeding on the Cross, I see
That divine and perfect Saviour,
Suffering, dying, and for me!

But behold! the Lord is risen!
And His whisper chides my fears,
Faithful friend and gracious Saviour
Through these long-past changing years.

Let me linger yet a moment
In that blissful realm on high:
Hark! I hear "Time is no longer,"
Welcome now Eternity!

Thought and spirit fail before it,
As the glorious scene I scan:
Lost in wonder, I adore Thee,
Son of God and Son of Man!

"JESUS IS HERE AND YONDER."

"The Lamb which is in the midst of the throne shall feed them, and shall lead them unto living fountains of waters: and God shall wipe away all tears from their eyes."
Rev. vii. 17.

"I will not leave you comfortless: I will come to you."
John xiv. 18.

"JESUS is here and yonder;"
    While you are weeping for me,
I shall be gazing in wonder
    There, where no sorrow can be.

You in the valley below me,
    I on the mountain of light:
Say, would my loved ones know me,
    Robed in my garment white?

I, with the race run before ye,
    I, from life's fetters set free,
Shall enter the mansion of glory
    The King hath made ready for me.

You, where the billows are raging;
    I, with the last wavelet gone:
You, where the conflict is waging;
    And I, with the victory won.

You, a lone vigil still keeping,
  And I, all my tears wiped away ;
You, in the midnight still weeping,
  And I, in the glory of day.

Still, do your tears flow the faster?
  Yet tears to these partings belong !
But think of the smile of the Master,
  The rapture of heaven's own song.

"Jesus is here and yonder ;"
  Here, where you patiently wait ;
There, where death never can sunder,
  Or spirit be desolate.

Remember, your bark He is steering,
  While safe in the harbour I rest,
Till the Lord of the glory, appearing,
  Shall gather His own to His breast !

RETROSPECTION.

"Thou shalt remember all the way which the Lord thy God led thee."—Deut. viii. 2.
"Cast not away therefore your confidence, which hath great recompence of reward."—Heb. x. 35.

HE was better to me than all my hopes,
   He was better than all my fears;
He made a bridge of my broken works,
   And a rainbow of my tears.
The billows that guarded my sea-girt path
   Carried my Lord on their crest;
When I dwell on the days of my wilderness march,
   I lean on His love for the rest.

He emptied my hands of my treasured store,
   And His covenant Love revealed;
There was not a wound in my aching heart
   But the balm of His breath hath healed.
Oh! tender and true was the chastening sore,
   In wisdom that taught and tried;
Till the soul that He sought was trusting in Him,
   And nothing on earth beside.

There is light for me on the trackless wild,
   As the wonders of old I trace;
When the God of the whole earth went before
   To search me a resting-place.
Has He changed for me? Nay! He changes not;
   He will bring me by some new way,
Through fire and flood, and each crafty foe,
   As safely as yesterday.

And if to the warfare He calls me forth,
   He buckles my armour on;
He greets me with smiles and a word of cheer,
   For battles His sword hath won:
He wipes my brow as I droop and faint,
   He blesses my hand to toil;
Faithful is He as He washes my feet
   From the trace of each earthly soil.

He guided by paths that I could not see,
   By ways that I have not known;
The crooked was straight, and the rough made plain,
   As I followed the Lord alone.
I praise Him still for the pleasant palms,
   And the water-springs by the way;
For the glowing pillar of flame by night,
   And the sheltering cloud by day.

Ne'er in the glare of the enemy's land
   He suffers His own to sleep;
The combat, the tempest, the raging wave,
   Tell His wondrous works in the deep.
The treasures of darkness, in secret hid,
   Can the child of the Kingdom proclaim:
Oh! tell forth the praise of Jehovah to-day,
   Give glory anew to His name.

Never a watch on the dreariest halt,
   But some promise of love endears;
I read from the past my future shall be
   Far better than all my fears.
Like the golden pot of the wilderness bread,
   Laid up with the blossoming rod,
All safe in the ark with the Law of the Lord,
   Is the covenant care of my God.

GOD KNOWS BEST.

"Your Father knoweth that ye have need of these things."
Luke xii. 30.

I WOULD have asked a smoother road,
   A summer sky and cloudless seas,
As sailors in the tempest loud
   Sigh for the gentle ambient breeze.
God knew my heart. Soul, take thy rest!
God chose thy portion—God knows best.

I would have asked a household hearth,
   And children clinging to my knee;
A faithful arm on which to lean:
   And yet have lived to work for Thee.
I would have made a pleasant nest;
But God has spoiled it—God knows best.

I would have asked unbroken ease,
   And loving friends, and home, and health:
He gave me better far than these;
   For, taking all, He gave Himself.
And now, if e'er with grief opprest,
I praise His wisdom—God knew best.

Now, what He wills, I suffer here;
  I know He giveth strength to bear:
And what He gives I will not fear,
  For He my joy and pain will share.
Come good, come ill, I take my rest
On Christ my Wisdom—God knows best.

IN MEMORIAM

THE LADY MARGARET CARNEGIE.

"She is not dead, but sleepeth."—*Luke* viii. 52.

WE leave, Lord, in Thy keeping
  Her precious dust; 'twill be
Safe where Thy saints are sleeping,
  And still o'erwatched by Thee.
While the sweet bird from her prison
  Soars to her Saviour free.

Thy mercy, past all measure,
  Thy love, so strong and deep,
Hath garnered safe our treasure
  That we so longed to keep.
We give Thee back Thy loan, Lord,
  And praise Thee while we weep.

Safe from the tribulation,
  From sorrow's rust and care,
From the subtle world's temptation,
  No more to shrink (or share),
She rests in Thy bright presence :
  Lord ! we would leave her there.

No fretting moth can reach her
  In the land where Thou dost reign ;
Sweet lessons Thou wilt teach her
  Before we meet again—
Raised like to Thee in glory,
  In robes without a stain.

Keep, Lord, our treasure !   Keep her !
  Though our hearts are sore to-day,
Thou knowest while we weep her,
  We would not say Thee " Nay :"
For the free bird's song is ringing
  In the land of endless day.

A VOICE FROM MANY WATERS.*

"Better is a poor and a wise child than an old and foolish king, who will no more be admonished."—*Eccles.* iv. 13.

HE listened to the voices
   That made the rushing tide,
Fed by the melting snow-wreaths
   The sparkling rills supplied.
The water-floods were roaring,
   And the sunlight on the spray
Marked where the rapid Passer
   Went bounding on its way.

Far in the dark pine forests
   That crown the mountain's brow
The woodman's axe has sounded,
   And many a tree lies low;

---

* Through the Alpine valley of Meran rushes the rapid river Passer; its force and brightness give life and beauty to one of the loveliest spots in the Tyrol. The mountains are clothed with pine forests. In the early spring, when the snow melts from the granite peaks above them, the trees are felled for firewood for the next winter's consumption. There is no other means of conveyance from these precipitous heights than the water-floods from the melted snow. The timber cast therein is borne by the rushing torrent to the river, where it is carefully collected by the Tyrolese. It is always a season of great interest and excitement among the people. Every tree bears on its trunk the mark of the woodman who felled it, so that each man has the record of his own labour.

Waymarks of my Pilgrimage.

Cast in the dashing current,
　　The forest veterans come
Down to the Alpine valley,
　　To warm our wintry home.

The bold, untiring torrent
　　Went shouting on his way—
"Without my help, good people,
　　You'd have no wood to-day.
I bring it from the mountain,
　　I cast it in the flood,
And the woodman's axe were idle
　　If I the work withstood."

"Nay," said a rippling streamlet,
　　"Your boast were all in vain,
Did the sun not melt the snow-wreaths,
　　And bring me life again.
Lost in the fern and mosses,
　　My silver stream were dry,
If the sunbeams ceased their shining,
　　And clouds obscured the sky."

Then the torrent leaped the granite,
　　Still foaming as he went,
And the streamlet followed noiseless,
　　On patient service bent;

And the pine-wood floated faster—
    For their labour was not done;
But he who talked the loudest
    Thought the service all his own.

Said another, "See my burden!
    Oh, if you only knew!"—
Then there came a gentle whisper,
    "I have a work to do."
"But can you bear the timber?"
    The torrent seemed to say,
"Or turn a mill so fleetly
    As I shall do to-day?

"You have no voice for singing;
    My work you cannot share,
You're such a tiny wavelet:
    What can a wavelet bear?"
And then I heard the answer
    Of the pleasant, murmuring rill:
Melodious was her music
    When the torrent's voice was still.

She said, "A wounded blackbird
    Paused on this grassy brink;
He had no heart for singing,
    But he stopped awhile to drink.

In a shallow pool I made him,
   He bathed his weary wing,
And early in the morning
   I heard him try to sing."

Said the cold and boastful torrent,
   "Is that all you can do?"
"Nay, 'mid the grass down-trodden,
   I marked a floweret blue.
It faded in the sunshine,
   And drooped above the tide;
I knew its root was thirsty;
   Ere night it would have died.

"I wandered gently near it,
   And kissed the withering spray;
See! it is bright and blooming,
   With six new buds to-day.
But dearer than the blackbird,
   And all the flowers I see,
Was a little thoughtful maiden
   Who bent last eve o'er me.

"She said, 'The stream roars loudly
   From many a mountain spring,
Yet this quiet rivulet
   Its own sweet song must sing.'

And then I tried to teach her,
  Before she taller grew,
That the youngest and the weakest
  Have still a work to do.

"The daily deeds of kindness,
  And words of truth and cheer,
Raise hearts like drooping flowers,
  'Mid withering sorrows here.
And many a weary traveller,
  Whose wounded heart may ache,
Needeth the cup of water,
  Given 'for Jesus' sake.'

"The thirsty ones are many,
  And mourners passing by;
There's room for e'en the poorest
  In love's sweet ministry.
A river flows for ever
  In a path no foot hath trod;
Its mingled streams make joyful
  The city of our God.

"There are thousand, thousand voices,
  And He who melts the snow,
Hears every song we sing Him
  Amid the waters' flow.

On from the Throne that Fountain
  Proclaims His mercy rife,
In living souls up-springing
  To everlasting life!

" So, little thoughtful maiden,
  Thy voice was not in vain,
And the wavelet bids thee welcome
  To her crystal home again.
Look from the rapid Passer
  For brighter streams above,
And learn a lasting lesson
  From her gentle song of love."

ALPHA AND OMEGA.

"I am Alpha and Omega, the beginning and the end. I will give unto him that is athirst of the fountain of the water of life freely."—*Rev.* xxi. 6.

 LAMB of God, I know that Thou art here!
Close as my clasping hands—nay, yet more
near;
And every sigh enters Thy gracious ear.
   I ask to see
More of Thyself, Lord Jesus; more of Thee.

Give me to walk with girded garments white;
The understanding heart, to read aright
Thy Word; Thy law, Thy will, my soul's delight,
   That I may be
More like Thyself, Lord Jesus; more like Thee.

Grant me Thy Spirit's might to bring the blind
To Thy dear feet, Thy light and peace to find,
And sin-forged fetters from the dead unbind:
   I ask to be
More like Thyself, Lord Jesus; more like Thee!

Grant me a ministry that Thou shalt bless ;
Give me Thy comfort for the comfortless,
And self-forgetful in each heart's distress.
   Oh, grant to me
More of Thyself, Lord Jesus; more of Thee !

Give me a baptism of glowing love,
Thy power and presence wheresoe'er I rove :
And my last prayer, all other prayers above—
   Oh, give to me
More of Thyself, Lord Jesus; more of Thee !

THE CHILD'S COMMISSION.

"I heard the voice of the Lord saying, Whom shall I send, and who will go for us? Then said I, Here am I ; send me."
Isaiah vi. 8.

BEHOLD a messenger, my Lord,
Awaiting now Thy gracious word ;
I only ask to speak for Thee ;
Look on Thy little child—send *me.*

Thou know'st the feeble babe I am
To tell of Thee, Thou spotless Lamb ;
My mouth and wisdom Thou wilt be,
And I a messenger for Thee.

Thou dost not seek an ancient name,
Nor years, nor wisdom, wealth, nor fame,
Only a willing heart to be
Thy Voice of Love—O Lord, send me !

These lisping lips shall then proclaim
The life and balm in Jesus' Name.
O Father, let me speak for Thee :
Send Thou Thy little child—send *me*.

Child, hadst thou lived an hundred years,
On life's full tide of hopes and fears,
Still of the Cross thy song would be,
And the shed blood that sheltered thee.

Reposing now on Jesus' breast,
Go whisper of that perfect rest
That waits each blood-bought soul, and He
Shall make a messenger of thee.

FELLOWSHIP.

"Call unto Me, and I will answer thee, and show thee great and mighty things, which thou knowest not."—*Jer.* xxxiii. 3.
"I beseech Thee, show me Thy glory." . . . . "Behold, there is a place by Me, and thou shalt stand upon a rock : and it shall come to pass, while My glory passeth by, that I will put thee in a clift of the rock, and will cover thee with My hand."—*Exodus* xxxiii. 18, 21, 22.

MY soul is dark and dumb! Why is it, Lord?
   Oh, when wilt Thou arise !
And, with the hand my many sins have pierced,
   Anoint my longing eyes?

My heart lies open to Thy searching gaze,
   My weakness, and my woe,
My sins innumerable, my failing faith,
   That only thou canst know.

Why am I sore distressed?—for Thou art nigh,
   And I would onward press,
And find some token of a Father's love
   E'en in this bitterness.

I asked to share Thy fellowship; to know
   More of Thyself, O Lord !
And Thou, attentive to my feeble cry,
   Hast proved me at my word.

I thought my soul would overleap with joy,
   More of Thyself to see;
I dreamed—to walk in fellowship divine
   Could bring but light to me.

I prayed that I might know Thee more and more,
   And all Thy will discern,
And lessons Thou wouldst teach me day by day
   Still patiently might learn.

I take the cup Thou giv'st; I know Thy voice,
   'Twill make my portion sweet.
I asked to share the path that Thou wouldst choose,
   And track Thy heavenly feet.

But when on earth no cloudless skies were Thine,
   No Eden bloomed for Thee—
But noontide travel, and the midnight watch,
   And dark Gethsemane.

And shall I only to Emmaus walk
   In goodly company,
And shun the woeful watch where Thou didst yearn
   For human sympathy?

Silent I stand before Thee, for the way
   Is strange, and steep, and rough;
Is this Thy fellowship, to "share Thy cup"?
   Then, Lord, it is enough.

Thy cup? Ah, Thou hast emptied it for me!
  It only touched my lip;
But Thou dost grant that taste to every soul
  That shares Thy fellowship.

The children's lessons, often sadly conned,
  Are seeds for future years,
And bear their bloom and fruit laid up for Thee,
  Though watered with our tears.

The goal is almost won, the river passed,
  And Paradise is nigh;
The shadow of Thy hand is o'er me cast,
  Guarding me tenderly.

Thou art so near to me, I feel Thy hand
  Shrouding Thy glory, Lord;
And in the deep cleft of the riven Rock
  I see—the Living Word!

Thy mercy and Thy goodness are in Him
  Whom I so dimly trace;
O God of Glory, in Thy Holy Son
  I now behold Thy face!

MY REST.

"The Lord is nigh unto all them that call upon Him, to all that call upon Him in truth. He will fulfil the desire of them that fear Him : He also will hear their cry, and will save them. The Lord preserveth all them that love Him."
Psalm cxlv. 18-20.

HOU art my Refuge, Lord. I flee
From other safeguard unto Thee.
Now on the breast of Love divine
Shelter this weary soul of mine.

Thou know'st the dangers of the road;
Thou seest the dark and foaming flood;
Thou hear'st my solitary moan;
Thou, Lord, canst save me—Thou alone.

Uphold my feet, so quick to fail,
And in Thy strength I shall prevail;
Go Thou before me, lead me on
Until our heavenly home be won,

And I for evermore shall rest
Upon my faithful Shepherd's breast.
How often hast Thou marked my track,
To bring Thy foolish wanderer back,

And from the brambles, where I strayed,
Lifted again my drooping head!
The secret of Thy care I see,
Because my Saviour loveth me.

Safe on Thy bosom I recline;
There is no strength but Love divine;
Thence spring life's peerless joys for me :
Where is my treasure, there shall be

My heart, and thoughts, and riches stored,
Safe hid with Christ, a costly hoard,
Till the wild thicket brighter grows,
And blossoms with the desert rose.

My Light art Thou, in life's dark way;
My Shepherd, when my footsteps stray;
My Buckler and my Fortress strong;
My Praise, my Joy, my Life, my Song.

Thy wisdom every day I prove,
And learn Thy endless, quenchless love!
By grace upheld, by grace restored,
Thou knowest that I love Thee, Lord.

THE LIGHTED VALLEY.*

"Whom have I in heaven but Thee? and there is none upon earth that I desire beside Thee. My flesh and my heart faileth: but God is the strength of my heart, and my portion for ever."—*Psalm* lxxiii. 25, 26.

SEE, the sun is sinking,
   And my pulse beats low;
Soon my breath will fail me,
   Fainter now I grow.
Come, oh come, my father!
   Raise my sinking head;
For death's darkening shadows
   Rise and round me spread.

---

* "In the afternoon the dear child, realising that she must soon go, said, 'Call my father.' When reminded he had gone to preach, she at once said, 'Oh, yes; I remember. Don't call him; let him preach; *I can die alone.*' She then said, 'Call Miss Fiske.' Her sister left her side to go for me, but the dying child remembered it was the hour of the prayer-meeting, so she beckoned to her sister to come again to her, and said, 'It is the hour when she prays with my companions. Don't call her; *I can die alone.*' So I was not with her when she died. Had I been by her side, perhaps she would not have seen so clearly the Lord Jesus."—*Life of Fidelia Fiske;* page 89.

Nay, why should I keep thee?
   Souls await thee now,
Darker than death's shadows
   Gathering o'er my brow.
Go! thy Master calls thee,
   And my work is done;
Leave me, oh, my father!
   I can die alone.

Call the friend who led me
   To my Saviour's feet.
Nay, it is the hour
   When around her meet
Many a thirsty stranger,
   Many a weary one.
Farewell, my beloved!
   I can die alone.

Christ is in the shadow,
   Father, Friend, and God.
Christ, the faithful Shepherd,
   Guides me through the flood;
Safe I breast the billows,
   All my fears are gone;
Farewell, ye who love me!
   I can die alone.

A BENEDICTION.

"Ye shall be a blessing: fear not, but let your hands be strong."—*Zech.* viii. 13.

GOD bless thee to-day with joy that never
    Shall fade, beloved, away:
Thine be the portion that endureth ever,
    Through life's long endless day.
Undying fruit shall spring from wintry hours,
    According to His word;
The rod shall blossom with celestial flowers,
    Laid up before the Lord.

Renew thy strength, and tread with true endeavour
    The path thy Master trod:
Safe! for His seal proclaims thee His for ever,
    Anointed with His blood.
Walk in the light, that every snare be taken
    That would thy foot betray,
And own—the love that called hath ne'er forsaken
    The wanderer astray.

A little while to wait for His appearing,
    And watch for Him to come,
And hear His voice of love, in tones endearing,
    Welcome His loved ones home.

From faith to faith still follow Him, though weeping,
    His lightest whisper heed;
Sow thou the grain, and leave to Him the reaping,
    And trust to Him thy seed.

Speak for the Master: He will guide thee duly
    To wield the Spirit's sword.
Live for the Lord who bought thee: serve Him truly,
    And He will bless thy word.
Thus all thy wealth in Christ the Lord possessing,
    Thy heart shall rest above:
Take now His promise, with my parting blessing,
    In token of His love.

THE CHILD'S MESSAGE.

"And the Spirit and the Bride say, Come. And let him that heareth say, Come. And let him that is athirst come. And whosoever will, let him take the water of life freely."
Rev. xxii. 17.

"CALL them in," the poor, the wretched, sin-
stained wanderers from the fold;
Peace and pardon freely offer; can you
weigh their worth with gold?
"Call them in," the weak, the weary, laden with the
doom of sin;
Bid them come and rest with Jesus; He is waiting:
"Call them in."

"Call them in," the Jew, the Gentile; bid the stranger
to the feast:
"Call them in," the rich and noble, from the highest
to the least.
Forth the Father runs to meet them, He hath all their
sorrows seen;
Robe and ring and royal sandal wait the lost ones:
"Call them in."

"Call them in," the broken-hearted, cowering 'neath
the brand of shame;
Speak love's message, low and tender, "'Twas for
sinners Jesus came."
See! the shadows lengthen round us, soon the day-
dawn will begin;
Can you leave them lost and lonely? Christ is
coming! "Call them in."

"Call them in," the little children, tarrying far away
. . . . away;
Wait—oh! wait not for to-morrow, Christ would have
them come to-day.
Follow on! the Lamb is leading! He has conquered
—we shall win;
Bring the halt and blind to Jesus; He will heal them:
"Call them in."

"Call them in," and swell the chorus of the angels'
song above;
Hark!—they sing a Saviour's glory, and a Father's
changeless love;
O'er salvation's sealed ones watching, though a veil
doth float between;
Holy Spirit, by Thy power, call—oh! call the wan-
derers in.

"Call them in," the Master waiteth; save them from
   the snares of hell:
Rest ye 'neath the blood-stained lintel?—of the grace
   that seeks them tell.
Hark! upon the crowded highway, and amid the
   city's din,
Sounds a child's voice, sweet and solemn—"Oh, be
   sure and call them in!"*

CHRIST REJECTED.

*"Whoso shall receive one such little child in my name receiveth
Me."—Matt. xviii. 5.
"They have not rejected thee, but they have rejected Me."
1 Sam. viii. 7.*

A MINSTREL went to a rich man's door:
He sued not for bread, nor for golden store.
Poor were his garments, and meek his mien;
The wise men never the like had seen;
The love that had found him taught him to sing,
And he pointed the road to his Heavenly King.

Fuller the song on the young lips grew,
And tender the burden, "Wilt thou come too?"

* See *Which Way? or, Fetch them in and tell them of Jesus.*

Men put him aside : I heard them say,
" The child is too young to have learned the way."
But bright in the sunlight the fair face shone—
" Christ is the way," said the little one.

Sweet was his voice; but the listeners hung
On the silvery chime, not the words he sung;
And wise men cavilled, " Can babes discern
What needeth the wisdom of years to learn?"
Meekly he smiled as he raised his head,
" Christ is my wisdom," the young child said.

They proffered him pleasures that fade and die,
He sang of his treasure laid up on high ;
The rich man laughs at the infant's words,
And turns again to his flocks and herds,
To his singing women and singing men,
To counting his gold and silver again.

A year rolls by. At the rich man's door
The voice of the child is heard once more :
He sings of the bliss at the King's right hand,
Of the judgment-bar where the dead shall stand ;
He tells of the might of the purple tide
That flowed from the heart of the Crucified ;

As the dying notes from the minstrel fell,
Said a careless daughter, " He playeth well ;

A lovely song is the child's last lay,
A pleasant voice have we heard to-day :
We let him stand at the open door,
But he made me weep—I will hear no more."

The wine-cup sparkled, the harp-strings rang,
And drowned in their mirth were the words he sang ;
Then, fierce in their wrath, they bade him begone.
No more in their midst sings the little one ;
The rich man jeered, and the wise man smiled,
And scorned *Thee*, Christ, in Thy little child.

Silence is there where the song hath been,
And a vacant place where the child was seen ;
Vainly we picture his home of love,
And follow the flight of the nestling dove ;
But, Father, how sweet will Thy whisper be,
"In my little child ye received Me."

LONDON: MORGAN AND SCOTT,
PATERNOSTER BUILDINGS.

www.ingramcontent.com/pod-product-compliance
Lightning Source LLC
Chambersburg PA
CBHW030306170426
43202CB00009B/890